An
expert
guide
to

Retirement

Ciaran Rea

APFS, MSc, BA Hons, ATT

Glenn Welby

FPFS, TEP

Design, typesetting and publishing by UK Book Publishing

www.ukbookpublishing.com

ISBN: 978-1-916572-70-6

An
expert
guide
to

Retirement

Contents

Preface

We have always wanted to write a book, and we hoped to gain a great sense of achievement and satisfaction in doing so, especially a book which people might find helpful.

Having worked as financial advisors for over 15 years each, we have built up a wealth of practical experience in helping clients through their retirement journey. As such, we feel well qualified to write a book on retirement planning. We genuinely want to share all the knowledge we have accumulated over those years, especially as it is a subject about which we are passionate and a topic which we know most people find daunting.

No matter what part of the economic cycle we are in and regardless of what's going on in the world around us, when it comes to financial advice and retirement planning, people generally ask the same questions.

Prompted by having more time on our hands due to the Covid-19 pandemic forcing us all to work from home, we took the plunge and decided to start writing a book on planning for retirement. We just felt that it would be a great idea to put what we do on a daily basis into a book format so it could act as a guide for people looking for help, guidance or advice on the subject.

We would get great pleasure knowing that this book helped even a few people, but more importantly we hope that writing this book will be something that our children will be proud of and maybe even something they could benefit from in future years.

Introduction

The average working life of someone living in the UK is currently 39.4 years. This is 3.5 years longer than the European average. [1]

During a lifetime most people face a series of continuous financial challenges.

This starts with buying a first home; the average age is now 31 years old. [2] This has slowly increased over the past decade, fuelled by growth in property prices which continue to increase faster than our earnings. [3]

The average age of becoming a parent in the most recent ONS survey for England & Wales is age 30 for a female and 33 for a male. [4]

It is hardly surprising based on these figures that we are not only having children later but also that family sizes have reduced. [5]

So, what has all this got to do with retirement?

As these challenges become more expensive our retirement ages continue to get later in life. For most, we spend a large portion of our lifetime worrying about financial challenges and how we are going to afford them. This book aims to help you understand how much you need to save for your retirement.

For those who have retired or are approaching retirement this book offers a sense check to ensure you don't get carried away with this newfound wealth and freedom. Overspending in the earlier years can lead to serious implications in the later part of retirement.

Chapter 1

How much do I need in retirement?

"Failing to prepare is preparing to fail." **Ben Franklin**

The pension and retirement landscape has changed dramatically over the past 10 years. Auto enrolment was introduced in 2012 which has resulted in 10 million employees now saving into their workplace pension. Another major change was pension freedoms introduced in April 2015 which effectively gave individuals much more choice and flexibility with their pensions at retirement.

April 2016 saw the introduction of the new flat rate state pension, and in November 2018 women's state pension was controversially increased to age 65 in line with men.

In addition, over the past 20 years, we have seen the gradual demise of defined benefit pensions, where your pension at retirement was linked to your salary approaching retirement and your length of service.

These 'gold plated' defined benefit pensions have gradually been replaced by defined contribution pensions where your pension is invested into a pot and what you get back at retirement is determined by the performance of the underlying investments and the amount you save into this pot.

Therefore, as defined benefit pensions would have historically been very common in the workplace, most people wouldn't have needed to give their retirement too much thought.

An individual knew that whenever they retired they would receive a certain percentage of their salary, usually half or two thirds.

In addition, they would know that they had their state pension to look forward to at their state pension age.

However, the shift from defined benefit to defined contribution pensions means that individuals are increasingly responsible for their own retirement income.

Individuals are now having to make their own investment decisions and take much more ownership of their pension provision and retirement plan.

This is a fairly daunting task and as a result more people are seeking professional advice to help guide and assist them through this process.

How much do I need to save for retirement?

Consequently, two common questions that are frequently asked with regards to retirement planning are;

1. How much do I need in retirement?
2. How much do I need to save for my retirement?

The two questions are interlinked and the answer to both questions depends on factors such as your age, how much you earn, when you would like to retire and, perhaps most importantly, what standard of living you would like in retirement.

The first misconception is that you need the same level of income in retirement that you are or were earning during your working life. This is unlikely to be the case. For example:

- Your mortgage is likely to be paid off by the time you reach retirement;

- It is likely that your children will be financially independent by this stage, which should result in reduced regular costs such as heating, electricity and food;

- If you retire at your state pension age, you will no longer be paying national insurance contributions;

- Once retired, you may be saving on work-related costs such as commuting and buying work clothes etc;

- You will no longer be making contributions to your pension as you will now be drawing an income from it;

- If you are a regular saver, it is less likely that you will continue to save on a regular basis in retirement as you may start using your savings.

Although not all of these reductions in expenditure will apply to everyone, it is probable that at least some will apply in some capacity for the majority of retirees.

Many studies have been carried out with regards to how much you will need in retirement.

The level of income an individual or couple will need will of course be based on their personal circumstances.

A broad rule of thumb used to be that to roughly maintain your current standard of living in retirement you will need around two thirds of your gross pre-retirement income. For example, if you are earning c£30,000 gross per annum whilst working, you will need c£20,000 per annum in retirement.

However, a recent study by the Pensions and Lifetime Savings Association (PLSA), aimed to set out a new set of 'retirement living standards' in the UK [6].

	MINIMUM	MODERATE	COMFORTABLE
SINGLE	£10,200 a year	£20,200 a year	£33,000 a year
WHAT STANDARD OF LIVING COULD YOU HAVE?	Covers all your needs, with some left over for fun	More financial security and flexibility	More financial freedom and some luxuries
HOUSE	DIY maintenance and decorating one room a year.	Some help with maintenance and decorating each year.	Replace kitchen and bathroom every 10/15 years.
FOOD & DRINK	A £38 weekly food shop.	A £46 weekly food shop.	A £56 weekly food shop.
TRANSPORT	No car.	3-year old car replaced every 10 years.	2-year old car replaced every five years.
HOLIDAYS & LEISURE	A week and a long weekend in the UK every year.	2 weeks in Europe and a long weekend in the UK every year.	3 weeks in Europe every year.
CLOTHING & PERSONAL	£460 for clothing and footwear each year.	£750 for clothing and footwear each year.	£1,000 - £1,500 for clothing and footwear each year.
HELPING OTHERS	£10 for each birthday present.	£30 for each birthday present.	£50 for each birthday present.

	MINIMUM	MODERATE	COMFORTABLE
COUPLE	£15,700 a year	£29,100 a year	£47,500 a year
WHAT STANDARD OF LIVING COULD YOU HAVE?	Covers all your needs, with some left over for fun	More financial security and flexibility	More financial freedom and some luxuries
🏠 HOUSE	DIY maintenance and decorating one room a year.	Some help with maintenance and decorating each year.	Replace kitchen and bathroom every 10/15 years.
🍴 FOOD & DRINK	A £67 weekly food shop.	A £74 weekly food shop.	A £91 weekly food shop.
🚗 TRANSPORT	No car.	3-year old car replaced every 10 years.	Two cars, each replaced every five years.
🏖 HOLIDAYS & LEISURE	A week and a long weekend in the UK every year.	2 weeks in Europe and a long weekend in the UK every year.	3 weeks in Europe every year.
👕 CLOTHING & PERSONAL	£460 per person for clothing and footwear each year.	£750 per person for clothing and footwear each year.	Up to £1,500 per person for clothing and footwear each year.
🎁 HELPING OTHERS	£10 for each birthday present.	£30 for each birthday present.	£50 for each birthday present.

The study found that in order to enjoy a comfortable retirement, an individual would need c£33,000 per annum, which equates to c£2,750 per month (this translates to £47,500 per annum or £3,958 per month for a couple).

The aim of this research is to provide some guidance and help people better engage with their retirement savings.

The report broke down how much is needed in order to live three different lifestyles in retirement;

- A <u>Minimum</u> Lifestyle – paying for essentials such as groceries, housing payments, transport, utilities, a one-week holiday per year and a moderate amount left to pay for clothing.

- A <u>Moderate</u> Lifestyle – paying for all the essentials and some luxuries such as a two-week continental holiday per year, eating out, with some left over for clothing.

- A <u>Comfortable</u> Lifestyle – again paying for all the essentials, hobbies and eating out, and either a long-haul trip or a three-week European holiday per year, and a comfortable amount left over for clothing, and a new car every five years..

The study (see table below) shows how much annual income would be required for both a single person and also a retired couple to live a minimum, moderate and comfortable retirement.

It is most likely that for most individuals and couples, aiming for a moderate retirement is a realistic target for retirement.

	Minimum Lifestyle	Moderate Lifestyle	Comfortable Lifestyle
Single person	£10,200pa	£20,200pa	£33,000pa
Couple	£15,700pa	£29,100pa	£47,500pa

It is interesting to note that £20,200 per annum will allow an individual to enjoy a moderate lifestyle in retirement which is roughly two thirds of the average UK national wage of £30,420 in 2019 [7].

This in turn would be consistent with the general rule of thumb that living off two thirds of your pre-retirement income will allow you to generally maintain the same standard of living in retirement.

Another point to consider is that income needs may change during retirement. People generally spend more money in the early years of retirement. This is frequently referred to as 'the golden years', as retirees usually have good health and plenty of time to allow them to enjoy their freedom and spend more by perhaps travelling and treating themselves. Later on in retirement, people will usually settle down more and spend less money on travelling and eating out but more on maybe health-related costs.

How much you will need in your pension pot for retirement

The next step is to calculate how much of a pension pot is required to provide you with any of the three different standards of living in retirement.

We will then assess how much you may need to save annually or monthly to provide you with these different pots.

As part of my analysis, I have made certain assumptions. I will assume that each individual will retire at their state pension age, which is currently age 66 (this is due to increase to age 67 between 2026 to 2028) and that each individual will receive the full state pension which is currently £175.20 per week at the time of writing (£9,110.40 per annum or £759.20 per month).

I have also assumed that each individual will take a medium level of risk throughout their investment term which will generate an average return of 5% per annum and that each individual will purchase an annuity, (I know this will not be the case for a lot of retirees).

An annuity is when a pension pot is exchanged for a regular income for life.

Even though not everyone will buy an annuity, looking at the pot required to buy one gives us a realistic idea of how much we need in our pension to provide us with a certain amount of annual income. Finally, I have assumed that all of an individual's retirement income will come from their state pension and their pension pot.

Size of pension pot required

	Minimum Lifestyle	Moderate Lifestyle	Comfortable Lifestyle
Single person	£33,000	£336,000	£724,000
Couple	Nil	£330,000	£887,300

The figures show how much pension pot is required for each of the three lifestyle scenarios, and is perhaps a reality check for a lot of people especially as the average pension pot in the UK is only currently worth £49,988 according to the Aegon's most recent retirement report [8].

This perhaps reinforces the point that if people want to live a comfortable retirement, due to the size of the pension pot required, they will have to start saving early in their working lives and on a regular basis in order to achieve this.

This also demonstrates that if someone is solely reliant on their pensions and their state pension to provide their retirement income, it may be unrealistic to expect a comfortable retirement unless they start saving at an early age and on a regular basis.

Interestingly, in order to achieve a minimum standard of living in retirement, a single person will only need a pension pot of c£33,000 and a couple won't need any pension provision. This is because the state pension (assuming they are entitled to the full state pension) will provide the majority of retirement income for a single person and all the income required for a couple in order to achieve that standard. However, the reality is that most people will want more than a minimum lifestyle in retirement.

It could be the case that retirees have other sources of income in retirement, for example, savings, investments, a final salary pension, income from a rental property, an inheritance, proceeds from selling a business or even downsizing your main residence or equity release.

The more sources of income an individual and/or couple have to fund their retirement the less they will need to save into their pension. However, for the majority of individuals, their pension and state pension will be their main/only sources of retirement income and a pension is still the best and most tax efficient way to save for retirement.

The above figures assume that everyone will take an index-linked annuity (meaning that the annual income rises every year in line with inflation), which is the most expensive annuity option.

Alternatively, if we assume that an individual takes a level annuity, i.e. the annual income from purchasing the annuity stays the same through retirement, the amount needed in a pension pot to achieve a 'moderate' or 'comfortable' retirement becomes much more attainable as the table below demonstrates. However, please note that the earning power of a level annuity will reduce over time.

Size of pension pot required

	Minimum Lifestyle	Moderate Lifestyle	Comfortable Lifestyle
Single person	£22,300	£226,000	£487,500
Couple	Nil	£222,000	£597,500

The above table shows that by taking a level annuity instead of an index linked annuity, the size of the pot required reduces considerably and as a result is more attainable and realistic (especially to achieve a comfortable lifestyle). However as already noted, this will reduce the real value of your retirement income over time.

Please note that although the income from a level annuity will stay the same, the state pension income will increase every year in line with inflation, therefore an element of your retirement income will always keep pace with inflation regardless of the annuity type chosen.

How much is enough?

We have established;

1. How much income is needed in retirement to provide a certain standard of living.
2. What size pension pot would be required.

The next and final step is to work out how much we need to save into our pensions in order to provide us with the pension pot required.

Size of pension pot required

Moderate retirement	
Single Person	Pot of £336,000 required which equates to £20,200pa
Couple	Pot of £330,000 required which equates to £29,100pa
Comfortable Retirement	
Single Person	Pot of £724,000 required which equates to £33,000pa
Couple	Pot of £887,300 required which equates to £47,500pa

How Much Do I Need to Save For Retirement?

Single Person – With No Pension Savings		
Age	Moderate Retirement (pm gross)	Comfortable Retirement (pm gross)
20	£199	£429
30	£315	£678
40	£534	£1,151
50	£1,123	£2,418
Single Person – Starting with £50,000 of Pension Savings		
Age	Moderate Retirement (pm gross)	Comfortable Retirement (pm gross)
20	N/A	N/A
30	£174	£537
40	£355	£971
50	£850	£2,145

Couple – With No Pension Savings		
Age	Moderate Retirement (pm gross)	Comfortable Retirement (pm gross)
20	£195 (£97.50 each)	£525 (£262.50 each)
30	£309 (£154.50 each)	£831 (£415.50 each)
40	£524 (£262 each)	£1,410 (£705 each)
50	£1,102 (£551 each)	£2,964 (£1,482 each)
Couple – With £100,000 of Pension Savings		
Age	Moderate Retirement (pm gross)	Comfortable Retirement (pm gross)
20	N/A	N/A
30	£27 (£13.50 each)	£549 (£274.50 each)
40	£166 (£83 each)	£1,052 (£526 each)
50	£556 (£278 each)	£2,416 (£1,208 each)

The figures combine the income you take from your pension savings along with the state pension (in the case of a couple, we assume there are two state pensions). We have assumed an average growth rate of 5% net per annum, i.e. after charges. The figures are shown in today's money, i.e. factoring in inflation which is assumed to grow by 2.5% per annum. In the above figures we have also assumed that anyone aged 20 will not have accumulated any pensions as they will more than likely only be starting off their career.

I have also included figures based on the assumption that you have already accumulated some pension savings and I have used the figure of £50,000 for individuals (£100,000 for a couple) as this is largely the size of the average pension pot in the UK currently.

Your monthly income should rise as you move through your career and as a result it is a good idea to increase the amount you contribute into your pension each year in line with your earnings.

If you are in an auto enrolment scheme, your employer will be contributing into your pension. This should be included in your monthly figures, which reduces the amount you will have to contribute personally to reach your target pension pot.

Under the rules of auto enrolment, a minimum of 8% must be paid into your pension, with 5% coming from you and 3% from your employer. As this is largely based on your salary, which should increase each year, your pension contributions (both employee and employer contributions) also increase each year.

Therefore, someone earning the UK average of £30,420 gross per annum will be saving c£161* in total into their pension each month.

*£30,420 - £6,240 = £24,180 x 8% = £1,934,40pa / 12 = £161.20pm

The reality is you will need to contribute more than the minimum 8% of your annual salary to ensure a comfortable retirement, and in some cases even a moderate retirement, or to have other options.

The best way to do this is by contributing more to your work pension, if applicable, and asking your employer to match your contribution. If this isn't an option then you will need to increase the contribution into your pension to ensure that you can maintain your current standard of living in retirement.

The figures show that the longer you leave this the more you will need to contribute, and the more difficult and potentially unrealistic this will be.

The reassuring thing is that although you may not be saving at the above levels in your 20s or 30s, you will more than likely have contributed something to your retirement savings and as a result you will not have to start saving from scratch in your 40s and 50s.

A rule of thumb used in the pension industry is that you should be saving the equivalent of half your age into your pension. For example, if you are aged 40, you should be saving at least 20% of your income into a pension. If at 40 you are earning the UK average of £30,420 gross per annum you should be saving £507 per month* to provide you with at least a moderate retirement. This is broadly supported by the above figures which show that a single person aged 40 (with no pension savings) needs to save £534 in total per month in order to achieve a moderate standard of living in retirement.

*£30,420 x 20% = £6,084 per annum which equates to £507 per month

Another commonly used rule of thumb is to aim to have saved at least 10 times your annual salary by the time you reach retirement. Again, taking the example of a 40 year old on the UK average salary of £30,420 gross per annum, they will need a pot of c£304,200 (£30,420 x 10) to ensure at least a moderate retirement.

The figures above demonstrate that you need to build up substantial pension savings in order to provide an income for a 20-/30- year retirement. Most people are unrealistic about or unaware of how much they need in their pension pot in order to provide them with a decent standard of retirement living.

The earlier a person starts saving into their pension the easier it will be to achieve these figures, as they will benefit from the compounding effect of the savings made in the early years working hardest for them.

This is best illustrated with an example which tells the tale of two fictional brothers, John and Peter, based on mathematical fact.

Example

John invests £100 a month from age 18 to 38 and then stops saving altogether. He achieves a return of 5% net per annum for the 20 years he invests. His fund continues to grow at 5% per annum for the next 27 years until he retires at age 65.

Peter blows his money on having fun, saving nothing until he is 38. Then he starts saving £100 per month until he too is 65. Peter also achieves 5% net growth per annum during the 27 years that he is invested.

At 18 both had nothing. When John reached age 38, he has pension savings of £41,000, Peter has nothing.

Now here is the point of the story. At age 65 John has £145,795 but Peter has just £68,219. So John has more than twice as much at retirement than Peter even though John set aside a total of only £24,000, while Peter invested £32,400.

The explanation is that John invested for 20 years before Peter got going and that early investment had another 27 years to grow in his pension pot.

People who start saving and investing sooner rather than later are effectively letting time and the impact of compounding do the hard work for them!!

Whilst the above example demonstrates the power of the compounding effect, it also illustrates why starting a pension as early as possible makes good sense.

In the early years of your working life the most important thing is to simply get into a savings habit by putting a certain amount away on a regular basis for retirement. For those in their 20s and 30s, they can start to get into this savings habit through auto enrolment.

Unfortunately, auto enrolment isn't currently available to anyone who is self-employed. However, getting into a savings habit at an early age is as important if not more important to these individuals. As such, it might be a good idea for anyone self-employed to try to factor in contributions to a pension each time they make a tax return.

Once you reach your 40s you should start to take retirement planning more seriously. People may have built up a number of separate pension pots through various employers, and the first step is to identify these pots and work out their value and if they are working hard enough for you.

At this stage you should be starting to identify when you would like to retire, how much you have already saved in your different pension pots, what your income needs will be in retirement and how to achieve this.

Once you know whether or not you are on track you can start to plan properly for retirement, and even though this process may identify a shortfall, this allows you plenty of time to build a plan to reduce or eliminate this shortfall and to make additional contributions if required.

Even if you can't save additional money into your pensions or savings to bridge any shortfall, at least you can now be realistic about what type of retirement you can expect and you can start to plan for this.

It's never too late to start planning for retirement, but having a plan in place will give you a much better chance of having the retirement you want and deserve. If you don't know where to begin, contacting a professional advisor to help you navigate you through the process may be a good start.

Chapter 2

Investment principles: risk and return

"Risk means more things can happen than will happen." Elroy Dimson

What is investing?

Investing is the process of putting your money to work now to provide a source of income and capital in the future, for example, to generate an income in retirement.

Investing offers the potential for your money to work harder, providing you with the opportunity to achieve better returns than cash over the long term, although this is not guaranteed.

As a result, the higher the return that is generated by an investment, the greater chance you have in achieving your financial goals.

Why invest: saving versus investing

Throughout our lives, we all have different goals that we need to save towards, for example, to generate an income in retirement, to pay for a deposit for a house or to pay for your children's university fees.

Saving and investing are ways to achieve these goals by putting money away now for the chance to have more in the future.

Saving

In general saving tends to be for the short term whereas investing tends to be for the longer term, i.e. at least five years plus.

It is a good idea to build up an emergency fund in cash savings which you can easily withdraw if you need to. This emergency fund should be big enough to cover three to six months' worth of living expenses if you are working or one to two years' worth if you are not (e.g., if you are in retirement). You should keep this money in an instant access or easy access account so that you can get your hands on it quickly in the case of an emergency, e.g., if your boiler breaks or your car breaks down.

You may also want a separate savings account for known expenses within the next couple of years such as a holiday or a new car. If you know that you'll need access to your money within the next five years, it's best to keep it as cash.

Investing

However, if you have a longer-term goal, i.e. five years plus, you may want to consider investing as the preferred way of growing your money and reaching your goal.

The main reason is because inflation can seriously affect the value of cash savings over the medium to long term especially in today's world of low interest rates (Bank of England base rate is 0.1% at the time of writing and hasn't been higher than 0.75% since March 2009) and this can have a serious negative impact on your long-term investment objectives.

Cash vs Inflation over five years

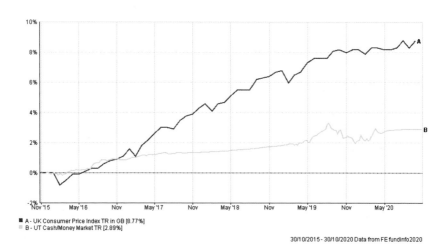

A - UK Consumer Price Index TR in GB [8.77%]
B - UT Cash/Money Market TR [2.89%]

30/10/2015 - 30/10/2020 Data from FE fundinfo 2020

Figure 1 above demonstrates how £10,000 invested in a typical savings account failed to keep up with cumulative growth in the Consumer Price Index (which is the most common measure of inflation) over the past five and 10 years.

The cost of living rose much faster than the money grew in a typical deposit account. The cost of goods that could have been bought for £10,000 in 2015 would have cost £10,877 in 2020. Over the same period, £10,000 invested in a typical deposit account would have grown to only £10,289. So, the buying power of the money fell by almost 6% in just five years.

Cash vs Inflation over 10 years

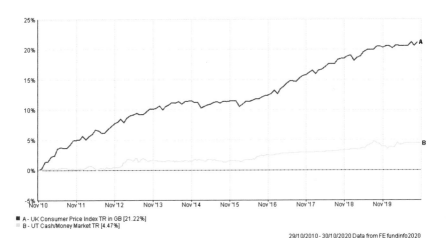

A - UK Consumer Price Index TR in GB [21.22%]
B - UT Cash/Money Market TR [4.47%]

29/10/2010 - 30/10/2020 Data from FE fundinfo 2020

If we look at the figures above over a 10-year period, the figures are more profound. The cost of goods that could have been bought for £10,000 in 2010 would have cost £12,122 in 2020. Over the same period, £10,000 invested in a typical deposit account would have grown to only £10,447. So, the buying power of the money fell by almost 17% over a 10-year period.

This simple example shows you the impact inflation has on cash savings over a longer period of time and demonstrates how cash struggles to keep up with rising prices. Inflation ensures that you will lose money in real terms and this can have devastating consequences in meeting a long-term goal or objective such as saving for retirement.

Investing provides the best opportunity for growth in real terms over the longer term. But unlike the security that cash offers, investments can fall as well as rise in value. Consequently, you could get back less than you originally invest.

Therefore, before you decide to commit to investing your money you need to be comfortable with the concept of risk and specifically with the fact that your investments will fall as well as rise and that there will be good years and bad years on your investment journey.

Setting out goals

In order to invest successfully, you need a clear understanding of your financial goals.

This begins by setting measurable and realistic investment goals and developing a plan to reach these goals. In addition, you will need to regularly review these goals to ensure that you remain on track to meet your objectives.

Before you decide specifically on what investment strategy is right for you, there are a number of important considerations that need to be factored in when considering your overall investment plan.

Item	Definition
Objective	How much money you need to achieve a goal, such as retirement
Time Horizon	The number of years you have to reach the goal
Risk Profile	The level of risk you are willing to take to achieve your goals
Net worth/Other assets	Have you any other assets or sources of income that can be used to help achieve your goal?
Savings Rate required	How much you can invest at the start, and regularly thereafter
Monitoring	How your goals are going to be monitored to keep you on track to meet your objectives

In order to make the above goals more specific, I have used the same goals in a real-life example, basing my figures on the information provided in Chapter 1.

In my real-life example, Joe Smith is 40 years old and is hoping to retire at age 67 to coincide with his state pension age. I have assumed he will be entitled to the full state pension. Joe is full-time employed and is on the national average wage of £30,420 and as per the general rule of thumb, he would like to retire on two thirds of his employed income as he will be mortgage free and his children will be financially independent at this stage. As such he will need c£20,280 per annum in retirement which (as per Chapter 1) roughly matches the income required for a single person who wants to live a moderate standard of living in retirement.

Item	Definition
Objective	How much money you need to achieve a goal, such as retirement – Joe knows that he needs a pot of £336,000 in order to allow him to live off two thirds of his current income levels (see chapter 1)
Time Horizon	The number of years you have to reach the goal – 27 years (until age 67)
Risk Profile	The level of risk you are willing to take to achieve your goals – As Joe is only 40, he is willing to take considerable risk for the next 15 years with his pension but intends to reduce his risk profile the closer he gets to his retirement age of 67 to protect and preserve his pension
Net worth/ other assets	Have you any other assets or sources of income that can be used to help achieve your goal – Joe will have his state pension which can be used to supplement his pension. In addition, he also has a paid up pension of £50,000 which can be incorporated into his retirement plan
Savings Rate Required	How much you can invest at the start, and regularly thereafter – Joe knows that he needs to save £355 gross per month to provide him with £20,200 gross pa in retirement
Monitoring	How your goals are going to be monitored to keep you on track to meet your objectives – Joe's pension and overall retirement plan will be reviewed at least once a year to ensure that he remains on track to meet his retirement goals

Now that you have an idea of how to reach your overall goals and objectives, the next step is to start building a retirement plan that matches your circumstances which is realistically going to help you achieve these goals.

However, before you start the process of building an investment portfolio for retirement, it is essential that you understand the basic concepts of investment risk and return.

The concept of risk and return/ the relationship between risk and return

People take risks every day of their lives. Simple things like driving to work every day involves risk, i.e. the risk that we may crash. Nothing in life is without risk.

But, we only choose to take additional risk if we believe that the reward outweighs the risk and investing is no different.

In investment terms we will only take additional risk if we believe that we will be rewarded in doing so. Most individuals will generally take some element of risk with their pensions because they believe that they will be rewarded with higher returns over the long term than they would be if they invested their pension solely in a cash account.

Every investment can be described in terms of the amount of risk associated with it. Higher risk investments tend to experience great volatility, which means that they are likely to go up and down in value more often and by larger amounts than lower risk investments. In return, higher risk investments have the potential to produce higher return over the long term, although this isn't guaranteed.

Everyone wants to achieve high returns by taking low risk; however, the reality is that if you want higher returns you need to accept that you need to take more risk and if you want to take lower risk you have to accept the fact that you will more than likely see lower returns.

Therefore you must balance your desire to receive a potentially greater return from a riskier investment with a lower return from a less risky investment.

It is important that the amount of risk you take with your investment matches your willingness and ability to take investment risk, and it is also important that you have some expectations of how much return you can realistically expect by taking this level of risk.

Understanding the risk and expected return associated with your investments is crucial and if you aren't comfortable with or do not understand the risk you're taking, you should not invest.

However, please note that no investment is risk free. As previously demonstrated, even cash deposits aren't without risk as they suffer from inflation risk, i.e. the risk of not keeping up with inflation, especially over the longer term, which can have severe long-term implications.

Before you invest

As previously mentioned, before you consider investing it is usually recommended that you have an emergency cash fund of between three to six months of normal expenditure (for those already in retirement this may be higher). This emergency fund means that you have some financial security if something goes wrong.

You should also avoid investing if you have short-term debts as many forms of debt, particularly bank loans and credit card debt come with high interest payments. It usually makes sense to pay off these debts as quickly as possible.

Asset classes

Now that you understand why investing is better over the long term to get your money working harder, the next decision is where to invest.

In investment terms there are generally four main asset classes, and deciding what asset class/classes are right for you can be a difficult decision as each class behaves differently in different market conditions and is associated with different levels of expected investment return and risk.

Cash

This includes deposits within banks and building societies and this cash provides liquidity within a portfolio. It is easily accessible but generally the more liquid the investment the lower the return. While cash has the highest degree of safety in terms of risk to capital among the four main asset classes, its returns may not keep up with inflation over the long term.

Bonds

A bond is an IOU issued by a company or a Government. By buying an IOU, you are effectively lending a company or a Government money. In return for the money it borrows, the issuer, i.e. the company or the Government promises, to make regular interest payments, referred to as coupon payments and also to return the original capital at an agreed maturity date. As the interest paid by bonds is fixed, they are known as 'fixed income assets or instruments.

Example

A 'BP 3% 2030' tells you that the bond issuer is BP, the coupon (or annual interest rate) is 3% a year and the bond will be repaid in 2030.

A bond pays a fixed rate of interest throughout its lifetime and its value will change when interest rates change. The value of a bond rises as interest rates fall. This is because although interest rates have fallen, the pay-out or the coupon from a bond remains the same. Therefore a bond has become more attractive relative to cash or deposit based savings. If interest rates rise, bond prices usually fall because the value of the fixed income has reduced relative to cash or deposit-based savings.

Example

if interest rates increased to 4%, putting £50,000 into a savings product would be more attractive than the above-mentioned BP bond as the 4% interest rate on offer with the savings is more attractive than the 3% coupon on offer with the BP bond. Consequently, the value of the bond will reduce in this scenario.

On the flip side, if interest rates fell to 2%, putting the £50,000 into a savings product becomes less attractive as the 3% coupon rate with the BP bond is better and as a result the value of the bond will increase to reflect this.

When you buy a bond you are exposed to 'credit risk' which is the possibility that the company/Government will be unable to pay the coupon rate or even worse the original capital, i.e. the IOU at its maturity date. Therefore, bonds are given an independent credit rating based on their issuer's financial strength, ranging from AAA (the highest rating and lowest risk) to C (the lowest rating and highest risk).

Corporate or company bonds are deemed to be of higher risk than Government bonds (called 'gilts' in the UK and 'treasuries' in the

USA), as corporate bonds represent loans to companies, so there is usually more chance of default – i.e. not getting your original capital back – with companies than there is with Governments, particularly those in the developed world. However, in return for the higher risk of default, company bonds usually pay a higher coupon rate than a Government bond to compensate the investor for the higher risk taken.

Bonds issued by financially strong companies and Governments can be seen as relatively safe havens. They are riskier than cash deposits, but considerably less risky than equities, especially during economic downturns.

Property

Investing in property can take two forms: investing directly in or indirectly.

Investors can invest directly in property usually via buy-to-let investment or purchasing a commercial property.

There are usually two ways of making money via direct property investing.

The first is via rental income which is expressed as a percentage of the purchase price and is known as the 'rental yield'. If you were to receive £6,000 per annum (£500 per month) rental income on a property that cost £100,000, the gross rental yield would be 6%.

The second way is through capital gains, i.e. the value of the property increasing over time. If you bought a property for £50,000 and it increased in value to £100,000 you would make a gross profit of £50,000. Please note that this only translates into actual profit whenever you sell the property.

Investing in property directly usually requires a good deal of work and ongoing investment which will in turn reduce your overall profit. For example, you may have the hassle of dealing with awkward tenants, rent arrears, damage and/or repairs to your property. As such, it would be prudent to put away some of your money each year to pay for the maintenance and general upkeep of your properties.

Alternatively, if you like the idea of investing in property but don't want the hassle of actually owning a property, you could invest indirectly through a property fund which is managed by an investment manager.

These funds usually invest in a number of different property types such as retail units, offices and factories which are then let out to companies who pay a rental income.

One of the big risks attached to investing in property either directly or indirectly is that it is a fairly illiquid asset class, as buying and selling properties can take a considerable amount of time, and it may take a while for you to realise your money, especially in difficult market conditions.

Therefore, if you do decide to invest in property, you should also have a reasonable proportion invested in other investments.

Like the other asset classes, the value of property can go down as well as up, although property investing usually generates inflation-beating returns over the longer term.

Equities

Equities, sometimes known as 'shares' or 'stocks' represent a share of ownership in a company. When you buy a share you technically own a slice of that company, so when it does well you do too and vice versa. If you own a share you can make money in two ways;

- Each year the company will hopefully pay you some of the profit it makes. It does this by paying out a dividend on each share, usually twice a year.

- The value of your share will go up and down but overall you hope the value will go up, otherwise known as capital growth.

Equity returns are influenced by a number of factors but the main ones are the underlying performance of each company and the wider economic environment.

During different phases of the economic cycle, some sectors/ shares tend to perform better than others. For example, during periods when the economy is doing well, discretionary stocks i.e. stocks that sell products/services that aren't essential such as airlines, hotels and restaurants and even car manufacturers tend to do well whereas defensive stocks i.e. stocks that sell products/ services that would be deemed essential such as healthcare, food and drink and utilities usually provide steady returns regardless of the state of the economy as people always get sick and we all need to eat and drink and heat the house!!

As already stated, making money on shares is dependent on capital growth from share price appreciation and income returns from dividends. However reinvesting dividends is the key to growing your long-term wealth.

This is due to a concept known as the compounding effect. This is where cash dividends are re-invested to buy further shares and start to earn their own dividends. Initially, the impact is small, but as time goes on the power of compounding starts to make a large impact on the overall value of your shares.

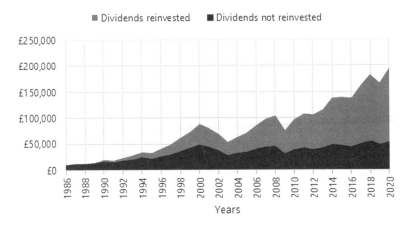

The chart above shows £10,000 invested in the FTSE 100 at the start of 1986. The orange line shows that if the investor had automatically reinvested any dividends they received, their investment would have grown to £195,852. The red line shows that this would have grown to just £53,394 if the investor had chosen to use the dividends received for other purposes. Therefore c73% of the total return over this period is attributed to reinvested dividends and the power of compounding.

This is also further supported by research carried out recently by Hartford Funds which shows that 78% of the total return of the S&P 500 Index from 1970 to 2019 can be attributed to reinvested dividends [9].

In summary, shares would be deemed to be the most risky of the main asset classes. However, they are usually the foundation of most investments for the simple reason that they have outperformed most other investments over a longer period – they are the most effective way of building your wealth and outperforming inflation over the long term, although this is not guaranteed.

The risk spectrum of asset classes

In UK investment terms, investing in cash and bonds issued by the UK Government (gilts) would be considered low risk.

Property, corporate bonds issued by UK companies as well as other types of global bonds issued by overseas Governments and companies would be considered as medium risk. In the case of global bonds, generally those that pay a higher income are riskier than those that pay a lower income level.

Shares in companies in the UK and other developed markets are considered high risk, while shares from companies in emerging markets are considered very high risk.

Alternative assets

Although cash, bonds, property and equities are the main asset classes, there are other alternative asset classes that do not fall into the traditional or main asset classes. They could include specialised investments such as absolute returns, private equity, commodities, derivatives etc or they could include specialised and rare assets such as art, antiques, fine wines and precious metals.

Alternative assets usually have higher costs and are less liquid (they are harder to buy and sell) than traditional investments and some of these assets can be complex and difficult to value.

However, despite these disadvantages, they can be very useful in a portfolio as they provide investors with the opportunity to invest in other asset classes, which they wouldn't have access to normally. Their main advantage is that the returns have a low correlation (they react differently to the same market event) with traditional investments especially in a falling market. This can be useful for further diversification purposes and may reduce the overall portfolio volatility.

How the asset classes have performed

There has been a lot of research carried out with regards to asset class returns over different periods.

One of the most comprehensive pieces of research is the *Barclay's Equity Gilt Study* [10] which is a complete guide on long-term investment returns, including data going back to 1899 for the UK stock market. The study provides the real return (stripping out the effects of inflation) from equities, gilts and cash.

It concludes that over the long term, returns from equities have been greater than those from gilts and cash. The study shows that shares beat cash 99% of the time if held for 18 consecutive years, 91% of the time if held for 10 consecutive years or 75% of the time if held over five years and shows clearly that putting money into equities almost always beats cash if you invest over the long term.

This is further supported by Jeremy Siegel in his book *Stocks for the Long Run* [11] which shows that the real return on a broadly diversified portfolio of American stocks has averaged 6.6% per cent gross per annum over a 200-year period whereas the real return on long-term US Government bonds has averaged 3.6% and on short-term bonds only 2.7%. Seigel argues that 'patient stock investors who can see past the scary headlines have always outperformed those who flee to bonds or other assets. Even such calamitous events as the Great 1929 Stock Crash or the financial crisis of 2008 do not negate the superiority of stocks as long-term investments'.

However, these average returns hide away from the fact that there can be large fluctuations in the performance of stocks from year to year. Although stocks generally produce greater returns over the longer term, they are also the most volatile of the asset classes especially over the short term and there have been years where you could have experienced large downward swings. Therefore although you would expect stocks to generate the highest returns over the long term, you would also have to accept considerable volatility as part of your investment journey.

Diversification

One way to reduce your investment risk is by using diversification, in other words spreading your money across different asset classes as you can still achieve strong long-term returns whilst not exposing yourself to the same level of risk you would be by investing solely in one asset class.

This ensures that all your money isn't invested in the one place. Whilst investing in one asset class or one sector could result in extraordinary returns, it can also result in considerable losses in a downturn.

By ensuring your portfolio is well diversified across different asset classes, you spread your risk exposure and lower the volatility of your portfolio – as not all asset classes move together in the same way; they react differently to the same market or economic event. For example, when the economy is growing equities tend to outperform bonds, whereas whenever the economy is slowing or shrinking, bonds often perform better than equities.

Diversification is the most effective tool against a single investment failing or one asset class performing badly.

A further form of diversification is by geographical regions and investing in different sectors. For example, even though part of your overall portfolio will generally have some equity exposure, within this asset class you can further diversify by investing your equities in different countries, i.e. some in the UK, America, Europe, emerging markets etc, and you could diversify even more by, e.g, spreading the element of your investment in UK shares into different sectors, i.e. banking, oil, utilities, technology etc. Then if something goes wrong with one share or sector, it only accounts for a small proportion of your overall portfolio and won't be too detrimental.

Example

I joined a global bank as an employee in 2005 when the stock markets were generally booming, especially bank shares. At the end of each year most employees were given the option of receiving a bonus either in cash or the cash equivalent in company shares. As the bank's share price was going up, most employees opted for the shares option with the view that the share price would keep going up.

In 2006 the share price was over £16 per share and for some senior Managers and Directors this was an extremely lucrative way of saving for their retirement as they had worked in the bank for a number of years, so the value of their shares would have (on paper) been worth easily six figures and these individuals were on track for an early and very comfortable retirement.

However, 2007/2008, the credit crunch took place and consequently share prices generally plummeted and the bank's share price plummeted from over £16 to 10 pence in a very short period of time. As a result the same Managers' and Directors' shares went from having a paper value of easily six figures to next to nothing and as some of these individuals didn't have a plan B for retirement. Their retirement plan went up in smoke!!

This is a good real life example of why you should not have all your eggs in one basket.

Constructing an investment portfolio to manage risk

The concept of diversification is further supported by Harry Markowitz, a pioneer of investment theory, who in 1952 introduced a concept known as Modern Portfolio Theory (MPT) which is still commonly used today.

Markowitz received a Nobel Prize in 1990 for his work on this concept, which introduced a new way to construct investment portfolios by showing how investments can be blended, using diversification, to reduce a portfolio's overall risk whilst still being able to produce strong overall returns.

Most portfolios feature a range of different asset classes mainly because asset class values do not necessarily rise and fall together.

The benefits of combining different asset classes in a portfolio can be demonstrated via a simple example as shown below;

Historic performance of UK equities, UK gilts and a 50/50 blended mix over a 20-year period from November 2000 to November 2020

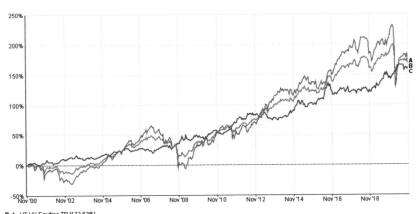

- A - UT UK Equities TR [172.62%]
- B - 50/50 UK Equities & UK Gilts TR [168.37%]
- C - UT UK Gilts TR in GB [161.61%]

27/10/2000 - 30/10/2020 Data from FE fundinfo 2020

Annualised return, volatility and max drawdown

	UK Equities	UK Gilts	50/50% mix of UK Equities & UK Gilts
Return pa %	5.04	4.88	4.98
Volatility pa %	12.59	6.23	7.55
Maximum Loss	-30.32	-6.03	-20.31

The table and graph above show that over the past 20 years up, until November 2020, a portfolio investing 100% in UK equities produced an average annual return of 5.04 per annum. However, it also had the highest volatility of 12.59% and a maximum 12 month rolling loss of -30.32%.

But, whilst the UK gilt portfolio produced a lower average return over this period of 4.88% per annum, its risk was significantly lower with an annualised volatility of 6.23% and a maximum 12-month rolling loss of -6.03%.

The benefits of diversification and modern portfolio theory is clearly demonstrated in the returns from the blended portfolio. A portfolio comprising 50% UK equities and 50% UK gilts produced an average annual return of 4.98% over the same period. This return is slightly lower than the 5.04% return generated by the 100% UK equity-based portfolio but the underlying volatility has dropped significantly from 12.59% to 7.55% and the maximum rolling loss from -30.32% to -20.31%.

Although this example assumes the portfolio had very simple weightings between the assets, it clearly demonstrates the benefits of diversification and shows that this strategy is a very effective way of reducing your overall risk whilst at the same time producing strong returns.

How much risk should I take?

Assessing how much risk you are willing and able to take is a difficult decision. Three basic questions need to be answered.

1. How are you able to deal with the ups and downs of investment returns, i.e. how much are you willing to lose?
2. How much can you afford to lose?
3. What returns do you require to meet your objectives?

Risk tolerance

This measures how much risk an individual is willing to accept with their investment.

A good way of measuring an individual's risk tolerance is to ask how much of a drop in their investments they are <u>willing to tolerate/accept</u> before feeling really uncomfortable.

The next step is to discuss how much of a drop the investor would have <u>actually experienced</u> in a worst case scenario, i.e. in extreme market conditions (based on a certain risk profile).

Typically, extreme market conditions would be during a stock market crash, i.e. in 2008 when the markets crashed due to the credit crunch, or 2020 when the market crashed due to the Covid-19 pandemic.

Example

A typical medium risk multi-asset portfolio dropped by c17.5% in 2020, therefore for an investor who would feel really uncomfortable with a drop of 10% or more, a medium risk portfolio wouldn't be suitable as there is a chance that in a bad year their investment could potentially drop by more than what they are willing to tolerate.

By contrast, for an investor who has a tolerance level of 20%, i.e. they are willing to accept a drop in their investment of 20% before feeling extremely uncomfortable, a medium-risk investment may be suitable, as even in extreme market conditions their investment fell by 17.5% which is within their tolerance levels of 20%. However, please note that this doesn't guarantee that their investment won't fall by more than 17.5% in the future; it just gives them an idea of what to expect, based on historical returns, in terms of a drop in a really bad year.

How much can you afford to lose?
– capacity for loss

Whilst risk tolerance assesses how much risk you are <u>willing</u> to take, capacity for loss measures how much risk you can <u>afford</u> to take. Whilst you may be willing to take a relatively high level of risk, you need to balance this with how dependent you are on this investment.

Usually the longer the time frame of the investment the higher the capacity for loss as you have more time to absorb any short-term downturns or market corrections which in turn gives your investment more time to recover from any short-term losses.

It is quite common for someone saving for retirement to take more risks with their pension in the early years as they will have time to absorb short-term corrections and their pension will have time to recover from any stock market downturns. Capital growth is their primary objective in the early years.

The closer an individual gets to their intended retirement age the more likely they are to reduce their risk profile as they may want to protect and preserve their pension at this stage. Capital preservation is usually the primary concern. Closer to retirement age, they will have a smaller capacity for loss as they wouldn't have much time for their pensions to recover if there was a downturn in the markets.

In addition, capacity for loss can also be determined by an individual's other assets. For example, an individual saving for retirement may have a final salary pension built up from a previous employment, guaranteeing an annual pension of £15,000 gross at their retirement age.

Consequently, this person would have a higher capacity for loss with their personal pension as they know that their final salary pension along with their state pension will fund the majority of their expenditure needs in retirement. They can afford to take more risk with their personal pension as they know that this is only required to more than likely fund non-essential expenditure needs in retirement.

In an ideal world, essential expenditure in retirement would be covered by secured sources of income such as state pension, final salary pension, an annuity, or even rental income, but this isn't always the case.

How much investment return is required?

Finally the third question that needs answered is how much investment return is required in order to achieve your goals/ objectives.

Even if an individual is willing to take more risk, it is always advisable to take no more risk than is absolutely necessary. Higher risk introduces increased uncertainty and ultimately may result in an individual not achieving their objectives.

In order to assess how much investment return is required to achieve your goals we need to firstly look at historical performance.

Although past performance is no guarantee of future performance, historical returns are often the starting point for projecting future returns. Therefore, you will need to work out how a typical portfolio (based on a certain risk profile) has performed in the past.

Please note that by using historical returns over a period in which the markets generally performed well and which didn't suffer a downturn, i.e. the period from 2009 to 2019, will result in unrealistic and unsustainable long-term return expectations.

You will want to make sure that the returns span long enough so that you can see how the portfolio behaved in both good and bad times. A period of at least 20 years would be a good start because historically this would incorporate at least one market correction/crash and as such gives a more realistic figure.

For example, based on historical performance, it is not unrealistic to expect a net return (after all costs/fees) of 4.5%/5% per annum on average from a medium-risk portfolio over the long term.

Therefore if you can achieve your objectives based on a long-term average return of 4.5%/5% per annum, you should never take more than medium risk even if you want to, as you are exposing yourself to a level of risk you don't need to take!!

Tailoring a portfolio to your requirements

Now that tolerance levels and capacity for loss have been established, along with realistic long-term expected returns, the next step is blending this all together into an asset allocation which is tailored specifically to the individual and their circumstances.

Ideally the asset allocation will generate the highest level of return for a certain level of risk or the lowest level of risk for a certain level of return.

This is demonstrated in the Efficient Frontier developed by Markowitz (see below) which shows a curved line with an efficient asset allocation for each risk level.

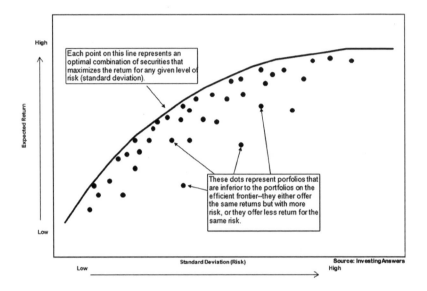

The allocations fitted tightly to the line are 'efficient' as they offer the maximum expected return available for each risk level.

By combining assets in different proportions, starting at the left with the most conservative (100% cash) and moving to the right with the most aggressive (100% equities), it is possible to tailor portfolios that historically would have provided the best opportunity of achieving the required returns at the lowest possible risk.

Holding a portfolio that is not fitted tightly to the line (the efficient frontier) could mean that you take a higher degree of risk than required to achieve a certain expected level of return. This would be unsuitable as most people would generally prefer to take the minimum amount of risk possible in order to achieve a particular level of return.

A successful investment is one where the end outcome meets your initial goals with no greater losses along the way than you were prepared to tolerate.

Once you and your financial advisor have agreed your risk profile, he/she will carefully select a combination of different asset classes, usually via a portfolio, to maximise the chances of you achieving your required returns within a risk profile and tolerance levels that you are comfortable with.

Your goals and in turn your expected returns and risk profile (tolerance levels and capacity for loss) may be different at different stages in your life and your asset allocation should reflect this.

An asset allocation designed for capital preservation, which might be associated with individuals who are close to retirement or individuals who have a lower capacity for loss, may be more weighted to lower risk assets such as fixed interest and cash, whereas an asset allocation designed for growth, typically for those who have a long time until their intended retirement age and/or a higher capacity for loss, may be more weighted towards equities.

To preserve the portfolio's risk and return characteristics, asset class mixes are typically rebalanced to the target weights at regular intervals, such as half yearly.

Example

We have 10 different risk profiles ranging from risk level 1 through to risk level 10.

Risk level 1 is the lowest risk profile and a risk level 1 investor would be invested solely in cash, whereas risk level 10 would be the highest risk profile and a risk level 10 investor would be invested 100% in equities, mainly emerging market equities. However, it would be very uncommon for an investor to have a risk level 1 or risk level 10 profile.

The majority of investors would typically be within the risk level 4 to risk level 6 categories. These risk categories would be invested in a mixture of equities, bonds, properties and cash with maybe exposure to some alternative assets for further diversification purposes.

A typical risk level 4 investor could be an individual who wants their money working a bit harder for them and are looking to generate long-term returns which have the potential to beat savings rates, or they may be an investor who is close to retirement and who is solely reliant on their pension and therefore they want to have some element of protection in the event of a stock market downturn as they have very little time for their investment to recover.

A risk level 4 portfolio/fund (low/medium risk) would mainly be invested in low-risk asset classes such as cash and Government bonds, medium-risk assets such as both domestic and global corporate bonds and commercial property as well as some high-risk investments such as shares, but held mainly in UK and other developed markets. Small amounts in other higher-risk investments such as emerging market equities may also be included.

Risk level 5 is the most common level of risk an investor takes – someone willing to accept a medium-level of risk in order to generate higher returns to achieve a long-term goal and they are willing to accept some risk and volatility in order to achieve these higher returns.

A typical risk level 5 portfolio/fund (medium risk) would be likely to contain low-, medium- and high-risk investments, including money market (deposit-based) investments, domestic government bonds, Sterling corporate bonds and global bonds as well as commercial property and shares. The shares would be expected to be held mainly in UK and other developed markets, and also a small amount in other higher-risk investments such as shares in emerging markets.

A typical risk level 6 investor could be an individual who has a long investment term. For example, someone in their 40s who is saving for retirement, or perhaps someone who has enough secured sources of income in retirement to fund their day-to-day needs, and who therefore has reasonably high tolerance levels as well as a reasonably high capacity for loss, with time to recover from any markets crashes or downturns.

A risk level 6 portfolio/fund (high medium risk) would likely be invested in a mixture of medium and high-risk investments, including both domestic and global corporate bonds as well as commercial property and shares. The shares would expected to be held mainly in the UK and other developed markets, but there is also likely to be some in higher-risk emerging markets shares.

Active and passive investing

Another important decision that needs to be made whenever constructing a portfolio together is which investment approach to use. There are two main investment approaches; active investing and passive investing.

In general terms, passive investing is an investment approach which aims to match a chosen index whereas the main aim of active investing is to outperform a chosen benchmark or index.

Passive investing

Passive investing involves a buy and hold approach which will generally track a chosen index, for example the FTSE 100; therefore the returns achieved should match the returns of the index i.e. the FTSE 100.

The rationale behind this approach is that passive managers believe that it is very difficult to consistently outperform a market over a prolonged period of time and there is some research that supports this view. In addition, as passive investing involves tracking a chosen index, they have low ongoing costs as there is little day-to-day management involved.

Active investing

Active investors believe that they can beat the market on a consistent basis. They think it is possible to add value to a portfolio by exploiting and investing in sectors or companies they believe are undervalued and under-priced and/or avoid sectors or companies they believe are overpriced and will therefore underperform the market.

Typically, actively managed funds are more expensive than passively managed funds as there is more day-to-day management involved as active managers are making regular adjustments to the portfolio to try and outperform the market and this is reflected in the ongoing price.

The objective with active management is to produce better returns than those of passively managed index funds. An active fund manager focusing on large UK companies would look to beat the performance of the FTSE 100 whereas a passive fund would look to replicate the performance of the FTSE 100. However, the higher costs of the active fund could outweigh any gains in investment performance.

Typically the ongoing management fee for a passive fund could be 0.2% whereas 1% would be more reflective for an active fund.

Active investors hope the fund manager will produce a higher net return (after paying higher fees) than can be achieved by passive investment and the greater costs associated with active funds need to be justified by returns in excess of a passive equivalent.

In addition, active investors generally have the ability to invest more freely than passive investors as they are not tied into an index, which in turn allows them to better manage risk. They can minimise potential losses by avoiding certain regions or sectors or moving to more defensive stocks, especially during a market downtown, which can also prevent or minimise large losses.

Which approach is best?

There has been plenty of research carried out over the years on which approach is the best, and there are legitimate arguments for both approaches. The main argument is whether active funds produce the long-term returns required to justify the higher costs.

There is also an argument that there is a place for both investment approaches. We support this view by using a combination of both via a 'hybrid' approach which includes an element of both active and passive investing.

Supporters of a hybrid approach believe that an active approach may be more suitable in certain assets classes or regions where market inefficiencies exist through illiquidity or lack of information, e.g. in some emerging-market countries. This provides scope for active managers to manage risk better and add value even after costs are taken into consideration.

However, in well researched, heavily traded markets, in developed world markets such as America, UK and Europe, a passive approach may be the best option as it is likely to provide a return that is equal or only a little bit lower than the market.

Ethical/socially responsible investing

Another popular investment strategy that has really come to the fore in recent years is the concept of ethical investing which is also known as socially responsible or sustainable investing.

Ethical investing is the concept of selecting investments based on ethical or moral principles and gives individuals the power to invest their money towards companies/funds whose practices and values are aligned with their own personal beliefs.

Different types of ethical investing have become increasingly popular over the past two to three decades and according to data provider Morningstar, £27 billion was poured into ethical (or similar) funds alone in the first three months of 2020 [12]. This supports the growing evidence that ethically focused investing, which was once seen as a niche investment strategy, is becoming more mainstream.

The first ethical fund was introduced in 1985 by Friends Provident and today most investment providers will have their own version, although not all apply the same criteria.

Ethical investors usually apply either a 'negative' ethical investing criteria where they will avoid investing in certain industries such as companies involved in alcohol, tobacco, gambling, weapons and the military; or a 'positive' ethical investment criteria where they actively seek to invest money in companies that make a positive contribution to the environment or people's lives.

Historically the common view would have been that if you were to invest in ethical funds, you would in turn, give up the opportunity to achieve the same returns you would achieve in traditional investments due to there being less choice available, which consequently leads to weaker overall returns.

As such, there would be a trade-off between the investor's desire to achieve strong returns versus their underlying beliefs.

Research carried out recently by Morningstar [12], in which they examined 745 sustainable funds and compared them to 4,150 traditional funds, found that the sustainable funds outperformed the traditional funds in all categories – over a 10-year period (up until 2020), the average annual return for a sustainable fund invested in large global companies has been 6.9% per annum, whereas a traditionally invested fund has made 6.3% per annum.

Some experts would argue that this outperformance is due to the fact that many sectors that are popular amongst ethical investors, such as US tech stocks, have performed strongly during this period, whereas sectors that would be historically unpopular or even avoided by ethically minded investors, such as oil, gas and coal companies, have under-performed.

Whether you agree with this argument or not, these figures demonstrate that there is less chance of there being a performance trade-off with ethical/sustainable funds versus traditional investments, and as ethical type investing is now becoming more mainstream, it is becoming increasingly possible to build a diversified portfolio that is both profitable and reflects your values.

Ongoing reviews

It is important that you regularly review your financial arrangements to ensure their continued suitability and to factor in changes to your circumstances and/or legislation which may impact you throughout your investment journey, so that ultimately you remain on target to achieve your objectives.

Reviews should occur at least on an annual basis.

If a portfolio isn't reviewed on a regular basis, it is likely that its asset allocation will deviate from its original allocation and your portfolio may become too risky or too conservative. If it is too risky, long-term returns may increase but so may losses. If the portfolio becomes too conservative, the risk may reduce but returns are unlikely to match expectations.

Rebalancing at regular intervals ensures that your portfolio remains within its agreed asset allocation and reviews give the financial advisor an opportunity to assess whether the fund is behaving the way it should be, i.e. how it is performing against a selected benchmark, and gives the advisor a chance to make adjustments if required.

In addition, the risk and return profile of an investor may evolve over time, i.e. in retirement terms, as an individual gets closer to their intended retirement age, and if they are solely reliant on their pension to fund their retirement needs, they may want to reduce their risk profile to preserve and protect their pension. As a result capital preservation rather than capital growth may become their main priority over time.

Investment summary

Finally, it might be a good idea to make up an investment policy statement (IPS). This is a document which takes your objectives (as per earlier in the chapter) a bit further, and now that you have an understanding of investment principles and the relationship between risk and return it should also incorporate your goals, constraints, investment strategy and rules for managing your portfolio.

This document is an ongoing working document which will evolve over time and which summarises everything you are trying to achieve and how you will achieve it.

It can help remind you what your long-term plan is and can also help you avoid acting irrationally or recklessly especially during uncertain market conditions.

I have provided an example of a real-life IPS, again by using the Joe Smith example used earlier in the chapter.

Investment Policy Statement

Objective	Joe would like to live off two thirds of his current income levels of £30,420 gross pa (see Chapter 1) at his retirement age of 67 which equals £20,280 gross per annum
Savings Rate Required	Joe knows that he needs to save £355 gross per month until his retirement age of 67 to provide him with a pot of £336,000
Return Required	Joe needs to generate returns of 5% net (after costs) per annum on average up until his retirement to achieve a pot of £336,000 which will in turn provide him with £20,200 gross pa in retirement
Time Horizon	Joe has 27 years until his intended retirement age of 67
Risk Profile	In order to generate 5% net per annum, Joe needs to take a medium level of risk and he is happy to take some additional risk for the next 10/15 years, maybe risk level 6, with the view of potentially reducing his risk level the closer he gets to retirement (maybe risk level 4)
Risk Tolerance Levels	As Joe still has c27 years until retirement he is willing to accept a drop of up to 25% in his pension; however, this will be reviewed on an ongoing basis
Liquidity	Joe wants to keep six months' income in instant access cash for emergency purposes
Taxes	Maximise his investment into his pension as it is the most tax efficient vehicle to save for retirement
Target Asset Allocation	Joe will leave this to his financial advisor but as he is willing to take more risk with his pension over the next 10/15 years, he would expect to see a higher equity content within his asset allocation to maximise returns
Investment Approach	Joe likes the idea of a hybrid approach to investing which incorporates both active and passive investing, as he believes that both approaches add value in certain sectors/markets

Ethical Preferences	Joe has no real views on ethical investing
Rebalancing	Joe will leave this to his advisor but likes the idea rebalancing on his pension will take place on a regular basis to ensure that his agreed asset allocation doesn't drift from its original allocation
Review Performance	Ongoing review to take place at least every year. Consider deselecting funds based on long-term performance not matching selected benchmark or unexplained short-term drop
Monitoring	Joe's pension and overall retirement plan will be reviewed at least once a year to ensure that he remains on track to meet his retirement goals

Chapter 3

Investing in uncertain markets

"The investor's chief problem, and even his worst enemy, is likely to be himself." Warren Buffet

2020 was a very uncertain and uncomfortable year for investors. The FTSE 100, the Dow Jones and the S&P 500 all fell by over 30% between mid-February and mid-March whilst both the Dow Jones and S&P 500 both had their biggest one-day drops since 1987 during the same period.

Therefore, it's no surprise that many investors were worried during this difficult period. It is a very tempting for investors to want to cash in their investments as no one likes to see the value of their investments or pensions fall sharply in value.

As a result, I spent a considerable amount of time, especially in the early part of the year, contacting all my clients, providing them with reassurance and answering any questions they had.

My message was simply to stay calm as history shows that over time values and prices should recover and make a positive return (although of course this is not guaranteed).

Volatility is part and parcel of the investment process, as prices will always move up and down in value.

Rather than focusing on short-term falls or downturns in the market, I reinforced the importance of continuing to concentrate on their long-term plan by focusing on what they can control rather than what they can't. Time and patience should always overcome the unpredictability of the markets.

This chapter is aimed at anyone feeling a little anxious. Hopefully it will provide a bit of help and reassurance and give you confidence in navigating the markets during any future rocky periods.

Firstly I would like to provide some understanding as to why investors behave in a certain way especially during uncertain times.

Behavioural Finance/Investor Psychology

The study of how investors behave is called 'Behavioural Finance' and allows us to better understand the decisions we make.

The basic concept is that having a better understanding of what we do and why we do it should result in better investment decision making and ultimately better investment outcomes.

Behavioural finance aims to influence and hopefully improve our financial decisions. It helps us understand the difference between what we should do and what we actually do in investment terms.

We display a number of subconscious biases in every decision we make, and whilst we can't remove these biases we can look to understand them better, and build a process that prevents them having a negative impact on each decision we make.

In investment terms, investors should focus on these biases that are most likely to impact their investment decisions as failure to understand our behaviour can come at a significant cost and can lead to poor investment decisions.

One of our main behavioural biases is 'Myopic Loss Aversion' which is the concept that we are more sensitive to losses than gains and overly influenced by short term considerations.

Investors are much more upset about losing a given amount of money than they are happy about gaining the same amount and we often struggle to cope with short term losses. This happens even if the losses are irrelevant in the context of our long-term plans and this can lead to investors taking insufficient risk in their portfolios.

This can also lead to investors cashing in their investments at the worst possible time and by cashing in during a market downturn, you are turning a short-term drop into a permanent loss which results in your investment/pension never having the opportunity to recover from this drop in value.

We are bombarded on a daily basis by information on companies, sectors and the general economy. Yet a tiny fraction of this information is relevant to our long-term investment goals.

In addition, investors tend to check their portfolios frequently, despite having a long-term investment horizon. Technological developments over the years have improved our ability to monitor our investments/pensions. However, this in turn increases the difficulty of sticking with our long-term investment strategy.

This is supported by recent research [13] which shows that investors who checked their portfolios more often than others took the least risk and more importantly made the least money.

The more frequently we check our portfolios, the more short-term we become, which in turn can make us too risk-averse. Viewing our investments and/or pensions on a daily or regular basis creates the urge to trade, often at the worse possible times!

Another very common behavioural bias is 'The Herding Instinct' which is the concept of following what others are doing and basing our decisions on the behaviour of others.

There is no better example to help us understanding herd mentality than in financial markets. Generally, the more we see other people doing something, the more we believe that it is the right thing to do, mainly due to the fear of missing out (known as FOMO) on something.

Investor psychology shows that people tend to buy stocks and shares close to the market peak whenever everyone is excited and positive. The same people tend to sell in a panic at the bottom of the market whenever the markets experience a downturn or a crash. This is the best way to lose money and goes completely against one of the fundamental principles of investing which is to buy at the bottom of the market whenever everyone is fearful and sell at the top of the market whenever everyone is being greedy.

Following what others are doing is a strong driver of behaviour and it plays a key role in fuelling financial bubbles and crashes. A good example of this behaviour is the internet/technology bubble in the late 1990s/early 2000s or the property boom in the early/mid 2000s.

People who had never invested before in technology stocks or in property wanted a piece of the action. They had read the newspaper headlines or they knew someone who had already invested in these areas – therefore, they invested their money due to the fear of losing out and this in turn drove up the prices even further in these sectors.

However, what they didn't know was that they were investing close to the top of the markets when the valuations were already close to an all-time high which in turn was actually feeding the bubble.

Unfortunately, a lot of the same individuals panicked and cashed in whenever the technology and property bubbles burst respectively, resulting in significant price falls and people losing large sums of money.

These are just a couple of examples of how our behaviour can have significant and negative long-term implications on our investment decisions, and this also demonstrates that we behave in ways that are inconsistent with our long-term investment objectives.

However, by understanding our behaviour and by applying the following steps especially during uncertain times, we can ensure that we make better investment decisions which will ultimately achieve a better outcome.

Have a long-term investment plan

To be a successful long-term investor, you need to set up rules and stick to these rules, especially during uncertain times, to keep your investment plan on track.

In times of uncertainty and in volatile markets, a good strategy is to go back to basics and remember why you invested in the first place.

Therefore, you will need to ask yourself questions such as;

- Why am I investing?

- What is my time horizon?

- Why have I chosen my investment strategy?

- Am I comfortable with temporary losses in difficult market conditions?

- How would I react in such situations?

Unless any of the fundamental reasons why you originally invested have changed such as your time horizon or your investment strategy, then you must stay calm and disciplined. Remember that you are invested over a long period of time and your long-term plan shouldn't be affected by a short-term drop in value.

Those who keep their focus and who remain patient during uncertain times are far more likely to be successful over the long run.

Often the best option in trying times is to do nothing, i.e. stick to the original plan and the original investment strategy – although small changes may be necessary such as ensuring that you rebalance your investment/pension on a regular basis to make sure that you don't deviate from your original asset allocation or risk profile.

Try to remember your medium to long-term objectives such as funding your retirement and try also to remember that any market downturns or crashes in the past turned out to be temporary even if they don't feel so at the time.

A stock market crash, although extremely uncomfortable at the time, looks like a blip over a longer period of time and this is further reinforced by the chart below which shows the performance of the S&P 500 since 1988 which incorporates numerous market crashes.

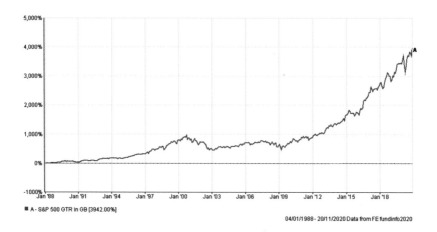

■ A - S&P 500 GTR in GB [3942.00%]

04/01/1988 - 20/11/2020 Data from FE fundinfo2020

The dot-com bear markets in the early 2000s saw the S&P 500 fall 49% and at the time this would have been a significant drop, spooking a lot of investors. But looking back over time, the falls were relatively small in the long-term context of markets.

The lesson learnt here is that markets tend to overreact in the short term only to recover over the medium to long term whenever the full facts are known.

Consequently, those who didn't react to previous market corrections have built considerable wealth and have more than likely achieved their financial objectives, whereas those who panicked and sold out during even one of these corrections are still in cash still waiting for the ideal time trying to get back into the markets.

It's important to remember that investing is for the long term and not to take a short-term view. Remember, if the value has fallen, it's only a potential loss. It's only whenever you decide to cash in your investment that it actually becomes a loss!

In fact, for those who are able to hold their nerve, this is exactly the best time to invest and/or to top up their investments, as values are at or close to their low and as a result there is much more scope for prices to increase in value especially over the longer term.

This is further supported by one of the most successful investors of all time, Warren Buffett, who famously quoted 'Be greedy when others are fearful, and fearful when others are greedy'.

We spend a considerable amount of time with any potential investor both at the outset and on an ongoing basis during annual review meetings. We discuss market downturns and market crashes to ensure that anyone who is invested understands that market crashes can and will happen during their investment journey as it is almost impossible to invest over a period of 10+ years without experiencing a market downturn.

This will allow us to gain an understanding of each individual's risk tolerance levels, i.e. how much of a downturn they are willing to accept in extreme market conditions, along with their ability and/or capacity to take risk, especially during uncertain times, to ensure that they are able to tolerate market downturns.

In addition, we use long-term return expectations (based on previous returns) over a 20-year period (as this will incorporate at least one stock market crash). We use these return expectations as well as incorporating an additional extreme stock market crash as part of a long-term plan such as retirement to ensure that the plan is prudent and realistic.

Taking this approach ensures that investors understand that their investments/pension will experience volatility during their investment term. This also helps them to remain disciplined and committed and to not deviate from their long-term plan especially during periods of market uncertainty.

History is on your side

History should provide some comfort for investors when markets are uncertain and volatile. Whilst it is very difficult to predict short-term movement in stock prices, long-term returns look much more favourable.

As previously mentioned, research from Barclays shows pretty clearly that putting money into equities almost always beats cash if you invest over the long term. For example, if you invested in shares over any 10-year rolling period since 1899, you would have beaten cash returns 91% of the time (75% over any five-year rolling period and 99% over any 18-year rolling period).

While markets can always have a bad day, week, month or even year, history shows that investors are less likely to suffer losses over longer period – therefore, investors need to keep a long-term perspective.

This is further supported by the below table which shows that the length of bear markets has typically been less than that of subsequent bull runs, with any losses sustained in the bear market eventually being recouped.

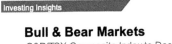

Bull & Bear Markets
S&P/TSX Composite Index to December 31, 2018

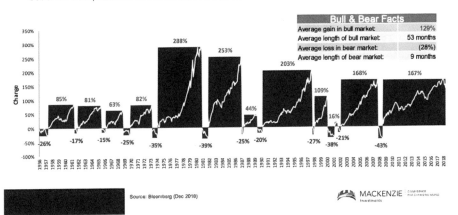

Source: Bloomberg (Dec 2018)

In the past 50 years, there has been eight bear markets (there has been 621 positive months and 123 negative months). In the intervening periods markets have undergone a bull run where they have increased in value from the bottom of a bear market. These periods have produced the best returns for investors.

The graph also shows that the returns in the bull markets outweigh the falls experienced in the bear markets and on average bull markets last longer than bear markets.

Therefore, even if you invested in the darkest of times, you could have generated positive returns if you had have invested for long enough.

For example, if you'd invested in the FTSE All Share just before the 2008-09 global financial crisis, you would have seen the value of your investment drop by almost 50% from peak to trough which would have been very difficult to take, and it would have been very tempting to sell at this point.

However, if you'd remained invested for the next five years and waited for share prices to recover, your investment would have grown by 31% overall (including the 50% drop).

In fact, there has only been one period in recent history where investing in shares resulted in a negative five-year return and this was during the dot-com recession. This would imply that length of time for negative returns is relatively short.

If we take this one step further and look at the figures for a diversified portfolio of stocks and bonds (which is more realistic for an individual saving for their retirement), the chart below shows that whilst the range of one-year stock returns has varied widely since 1950 (+47% to -39%), a blend of stocks and bonds has not produced a negative return over any five-year rolling period over the past 69 years despite the great variances in annual returns we have seen since 1950.

JPM Guide to the markets – US Q4 P71

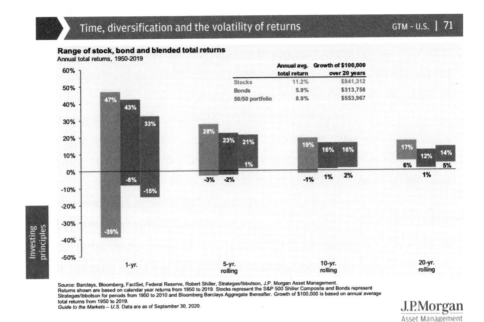

Range of stock, bond and blended total returns
Annual total returns, 1950-2019

	Annual avg. total return	Growth of $100,000 over 20 years
Stocks	11.2%	$841,312
Bonds	5.9%	$313,758
50/50 portfolio	8.9%	$553,967

Source: Barclays, Bloomberg, FactSet, Federal Reserve, Robert Shiller, Strategas/Ibbotson, J.P. Morgan Asset Management.
Returns shown are based on calendar year returns from 1950 to 2019. Stocks represent the S&P 500 Shiller Composite and Bonds represent Strategas/Ibbotson for periods from 1950 to 2010 and Bloomberg Barclays Aggregate thereafter. Growth of $100,000 is based on annual average total returns from 1950 to 2019.
Guide to the Markets – U.S. Data are as of September 30, 2020.

J.P.Morgan
Asset Management

The chart above also shows that investment risk declines over time as the range of potential investment returns narrow, therefore there is more certainty of returns.

Therefore, although historic returns are no guarantee of future returns, hopefully history can provide us with a degree of comfort and provide us with the evidence and peace of mind, especially during uncertain times, that time and patience should overcome the unpredictability of the markets.

Remain invested and don't try to time the markets

It is well known within the investment community that 'time in the market rather than timing the market' delivers the best results.

If you listen to the news or read the newspapers, especially during uncertain times, you'll hear a number of reasons to sell your investments. You will find that there will be plenty of investors that will make an impulsive decision selling some or all of their investments with the view to reinvest once the markets start to recover.

It is human nature to invest when things look good and to cash in when things look bad and history shows that investors tend to do exactly that.

This is further reinforced by the chart below which shows that most investment into US equity during the period between 1995 to the end of 2019 usually peaked close to when the market was also at its peak and investors tended to cash in whenever the market was at its lowest.

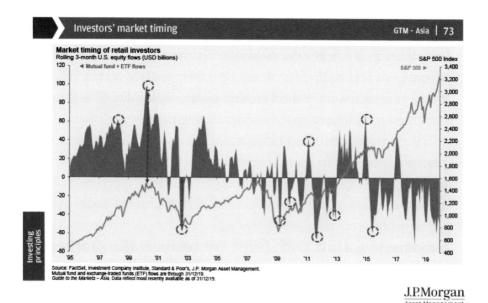

Consequently, investors invested when the market was at its most expensive and cashed in whenever the market was at its cheapest which is ultimately the best way to lose money!

It can also be very tempting to try and time the market. There are huge benefits of getting it right; however, it is very difficult to predict with any degree of certainty when is the best time to buy or sell.

With the speed that markets move, the risks of getting it wrong are very high and can have significant negative consequences on your investment. There is a significant risk that by trying to time your entry into or exit from the market, you could end up selling low or buying high with devastating consequences.

Research carried out [14] shows that the US markets have returned an average of 8.5% over the past 30 years despite the fact that we have seen a financial crisis, terror attacks and market crashes.

However, the average investor in the US stock market has only seen a return of 4.25% during the same period. This is mainly because they have panicked during the downturns and cashed in some or all of their investment and reinvested their money by trying to time the market. If they had have stayed disciplined and remained invested they would have doubled their money.

The same report shows the importance of having a financial advisor, especially during volatile markets. Research conducted in Canada has shown that that even just having a five-year relationship with a financial advisor can add 1.5 times wealth compared with investors who have no relationship with a financial advisor. Over a longer period, the performance improves to 2.73% over a 15-year period.

This value is added by the financial advisor not only by picking the right stocks or trying to time the markets but by ensuring that investors don't panic and simply remain invested.

The temptation can be to wait until the markets have recovered and then reinvest your money. However, some of the strongest returns are often seen just before and just after a downturn in the markets. For example, an investor who called the dot-com bubble too early would have missed out on a return of 39% in the two years prior to the market crash or a 19% return in the year prior to the crash [15].

Missing out on the best days in the market can have disastrous consequences for your investment and can significantly reduce your returns. The table below [16] shows that missing just 10 of the best trading days in equities in the FTSE All-Share between 2004 and 2019 would have reduced your annualised return from 7.6% to 3.3%. Missing additional gains over 20, 30 or 40 days would have been even more detrimental to your returns.

FTSE All-Share: Effect of missing best days

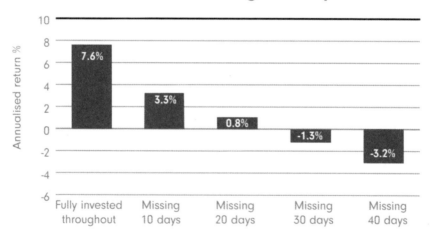

This is further supported by the table below [17] which shows that if you had have invested £10,000 on the last day of 1985 and missed the 10 best days of the stock market up until the end of 2018, you would have been £89,828 worse off than if you had remained invested the whole time. And if you had missed the 50 best days, you would have lost £168,030.

Please note that the reverse is also true and if you would have missed the worse performing days you would have been better off keeping your money in cash, but this would have required exceptional timing which is almost impossible even for a seasoned professional.

GROWTH OF £10,000 INVESTED ON 31 DECEMBER 1985

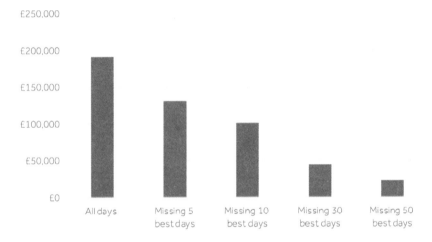

Hopefully the above examples show the pitfalls of trying to time the market and also the negative impact panicking in falling markets can have on your investments and long-term goals.

The best course of action is to stay disciplined, remain patient, remember you are investing over the long term and to stay invested. This is because by staying invested and weathering the storm, you are giving yourself the best chance to achieve your long-term goals.

Diversification

As already discussed in Chapter 2, diversification is one of the fundamental principles of good risk management.

Having all your eggs in one basket could mean that the performance of your pension pot is tied to one asset, which can have a particularly big impact whenever markets are uncertain.

Different assets such as equities, bonds, property and cash perform differently in different market conditions, as do different regions and sectors. For example, at the time of writing American equities have generally performed well during the current Covid-19 crisis, whereas UK equities have performed poorly.

However, by spreading your money across different regions and sectors, you can build a pension/investment that is likely to be less volatile than a concentrated one, i.e. only invested in one asset/region and/or sector.

In a diversified portfolio, whenever one part of the portfolio performs poorly, hopefully another part will perform well.

For example, take shares and bonds. Historically, shares have delivered the best long-term returns, but share prices tend to go up and down more than bonds. Shares are more sensitive to market events such as in a market downturn, whereas bonds tend to be less so. As such, bonds provide a more stable return when share prices are falling, limiting losses in a market downturn.

Diversification will give you the best chance of mitigating the more extreme losses associated with individual markets, especially in volatile times, whilst at the same time benefitting from the eventual recovery whenever it comes.

For example, the FTSE All Share dropped by 43% during the global financial crisis of 2008 whereas a typical medium-risk, multi-asset portfolio only dropped by 12.33% during the same period. More recently the FTSE All Share dropped by 36% during the worst of the Covid-19 pandemic in March 2020 whereas a typical medium-risk, multi-asset portfolio only dropped by 17.38%.

Rebalancing

Another basic investment principle is the concept of portfolio rebalancing.

Investors often create a portfolio with a specific asset allocation (which is often a mixture of shares, bonds, property and other asset classes) to match their risk profile.

According to several studies previously carried out [18], the majority of returns generated in an investment portfolio can be explained by its asset allocation.

Getting your asset allocation right is extremely important as a considerable amount of the performance generated from a portfolio will be determined by your asset allocation and getting this right.

Rebalancing involves the buying and selling of various investments within your portfolio to achieve a certain allocation by asset classes.

This is important because if your investment isn't reviewed and rebalanced on a regular basis the asset allocation can completely change, especially during times of market volatility, as some investments within your portfolio will increase or decrease in value more or less than the others.

This can result in an asset allocation drifting from its original target and may result in you taking more risk than originally intended as not everything in your portfolio will grow at the same rate.

It is likely that in addition to your asset allocation being different to its original target, it will also be riskier, as higher risk investments i.e. stocks tend to produce higher returns over time and this will result in too many higher risk investments being in your portfolio.

To ensure that your investment is aligned to its target risk profile and asset allocation, it must be regularly rebalanced. This process involves selling enough of the overweighted assets in your portfolio to bring them down to their target allocations and using the proceeds to buy enough of the underweighted assets to bring them up to their targets.

Rebalancing sounds simple, but in reality it is difficult to do because it is counterintuitive – you will be selling some of your best-performing asset classes and buying some of your worst-performing ones.

However, no asset class will continue to outperform on a consistent basis and this is further supported by the table below which shows the performance of different assets over the past 12 years.

Asset class returns (GBP)

GTM – UK | 98

J.P.Morgan
Asset Management

2008	2009	2010	2011	2012	2013	2014	2015	2016	2017	2018	2019	YTD	Q3 '20	Ann. return since '08	Vol.
Govt bonds 52.6%	EME 59.4%	REITs 31.6%	EMD 8.1%	REITs 18.9%	DM Equities 25.0%	REITs 26.1%	REITs 6.2%	HY bonds 36.9%	EME 25.9%	Govt bonds 5.8%	DM Equities 23.4%	Govt bonds 8.7%	EME 4.6%	REITs 22.0%	EME 24.4%
IG bonds 26.5%	HY bonds 44.2%	EME 22.9%	REITs 8.1%	HY bonds 14.1%	Portfolio 6.0%	EMD 14.0%	EMD 7.0%	Cmdty 33.2%	DM Equities 12.4%	HY bonds 2.7%	REITs 23.1%	IG bonds 8.5%	Cmdty 4.2%	HY bonds 11.1%	Govt bonds 16.6%
EMD 21.8%	DM Equities 16.4%	Cmdty 20.5%	Govt bonds 7.1%	EME 13.4%	HY bonds 6.0%	DM Equities 12.1%	DM Equities 5.6%	EME 33.1%	Portfolio 5.6%	IG bonds 2.4%	EME 14.3%	DM Equities 4.6%	DM Equities 3.3%	EMD 10.6%	Cmdty 14.7%
Cash 6.9%	Portfolio 15.8%	HY bonds 17.5%	IG bonds 5.1%	EMD 12.3%	REITs 1.3%	IG bonds 9.6%	Govt bonds 2.3%	EMD 31.4%	EMD 0.7%	REITs 1.8%	Portfolio 12.6%	Hedge Funds 4.1%	Portfolio 0.9%	DM Equities 9.8%	REITs 14.2%
Hedge Funds 6.3%	EMD 15.6%	DM Equities 15.9%	HY bonds 3.4%	DM Equities 11.6%	Cash 0.5%	Portfolio 8.4%	IG bonds 2.0%	REITs 10.4%	HY bonds 0.6%	EMD 1.7%	EMD 10.5%	Portfolio 3.4%	HY bonds 0.3%	Portfolio 8.1%	HY bonds 13.3%
Portfolio 2.8%	REITs 13.5%	EMD 15.9%	Cash 1.2%	Portfolio 7.5%	IG bonds -1.5%	HY bonds 6.1%	Hedge Funds 1.8%	DM Equities 29.0%	Cash 0.4%	Cash 0.6%	HY bonds 9.3%	HY bonds 3.0%	Cash 0.0%	IG bonds 7.8%	DM Equities 12.5%
HY bonds -0.1%	IG bonds 6.1%	Portfolio 14.8%	Portfolio -1.5%	IG bonds 6.3%	EME -4.1%	Hedge Funds 5.6%	HY bonds 1.6%	Portfolio 27.0%	REITs -0.2%	Portfolio -0.8%	IG bonds 7.2%	EMD 1.5%	IG bonds -1.5%	Govt bonds 6.2%	EMD 8.3%
Cmdty -10.9%	Cmdty 5.3%	IG bonds 9.2%	DM Equities -4.3%	Cash 1.4%	Govt bonds -5.1%	Govt bonds 5.4%	Portfolio 1.2%	IG bonds 24.4%	IG bonds -0.4%	Hedge Funds -0.6%	Hedge Funds 4.4%	EME 1.5%	Govt bonds -1.6%	EME 5.4%	Portfolio 7.6%
REITs -13.2%	Cash 2.2%	Hedge Funds 8.5%	Hedge Funds -8.2%	Hedge Funds -1.0%	EME -8.1%	EME 4.3%	Cash 0.1%	Hedge Funds 22.3%	Hedge Funds -3.2%	DM Equities -2.5%	Cmdty 3.5%	Cash 0.6%	Hedge Funds -1.9%	Hedge Funds 3.2%	Hedge Funds 7.2%
DM Equities -17.4%	Hedge Funds 1.0%	EMD 8.5%	Cmdty -12.7%	Govt bonds -2.6%	EMD -7.0%	Cash 0.8%	EME -9.7%	Govt bonds 21.3%	Govt bonds -3.2%	EME -5.7%	Govt bonds 1.5%	Cmdty -9.9%	EMD -2.2%	Cash 1.4%	IG bonds 6.6%
EME -35.2%	Govt bonds -8.0%	Cash 0.9%	EME -17.6%	Cmdty -5.4%	Cmdty -11.2%	Cmdty -11.9%	Cmdty -20.3%	Cash 0.7%	Cmdty -7.1%	Cmdty -8.9%	Cash 1.0%	REITs -11.5%	REITs -3.0%	Cmdty -2.6%	Cash 1.7%

Source: Bloomberg Barclays, FTSE, J.P. Morgan Economic Research, MSCI, Refinitiv Datastream, J.P. Morgan Asset Management. Annualised return covers the period from 2008 to 2019. Vol. is the standard deviation of annual returns. Govt bonds: Bloomberg Barclays Global Aggregate Government Treasuries; HY bonds: ICE BofA Global High Yield; EMD: J.P. Morgan EMBI Global Diversified; IG bonds: Bloomberg Barclays Global Aggregate – Corporates; Cmdty: Bloomberg Commodity; REITs: FTSE NAREIT All REITS; DM Equities: MSCI World; EME: MSCI EM; Hedge funds: HFRI Global Hedge Fund Index; Cash: JP Morgan Cash United Kingdom (GM). Hypothetical portfolio (for illustrative purposes only and not to be taken as a recommendation): 30% DM equities; 10% EM equities; 15% IG bonds; 12.5% government bonds; 7.5% HY bonds; EMD; 5% commodities; 5% cash; 5% REITs and 5% hedge funds. All returns are total return, in GBP, and are unhedged. Past performance is not a reliable indicator of current and future results. Guide to the Markets - UK. Data as of 30 September 2020.

The table shows that no one asset class consistently outperforms and there is no pattern to how any one class moves up and down the list from year to year.

All this table shows is the randomness of movements in different asset classes and that this movement is unpredictable.

However, what we can say is that strong performers eventually become weak performers and vice versa. For example, Government bonds were the strongest performer in 2018 but were the 2nd worst performer the following year, and developed market equities were the strongest performer in 2019 despite being the 3rd weakest performer the previous year.

This supports the well-known financial concept called 'reversion to the mean' which argues that no stock, or in this case asset class, can behave far above or below its long-term average level for very long, and that usually a period of outperformance is followed by a period of underperformance and that ultimately the long-term average will remain intact.

Rebalancing mightn't always work 100% the way you would like it but the number of examples where it works outweigh the number where it doesn't, because of reversion to the mean.

At worst, you may reduce your holdings in a strong-performing asset class a bit too early; however, it's highly likely that this same asset class will eventually underperform whenever it reverts to its long-term average.

In its simplest form, rebalancing requires the discipline to buy low and sell high which is one of the fundamental principles of successful long-term investing. It is a tried and tested way to generate extra return whilst at the same time control the overall risk in your portfolio.

Chapter 4

Investment vehicles for retirement

"An investment in knowledge pays the best interest." Ben Franklin

For most individuals who are saving for retirement, the most obvious option is putting money into a pension. This is a great way to save as it is tax efficient (more on this below) and if you are lucky enough to be in a workplace pension, you will receive free money via employer contributions into your pension.

Pension versus Property

Despite the tax advantages of saving into a pension plan (and/or an ISA) for retirement, property investment has become a very popular and successful vehicle for many individuals saving for their retirement in recent years.

For some people, concerns about the volatility of the stock markets and the appeal of owning an investment asset which is real and tangible mean they would rather invest in property to fund their retirement than save into a pension despite the tax disadvantages of doing so.

This is mainly via owning a portfolio of buy-to-let properties (but it could also mean just owning their own home).

Buy-to-let involves investing in property with the expectation of capital growth via an increase in the value of the property over time, with the rental income from tenants either increasing the overall return and/or covering mortgage costs (if applicable) and any outgoings.

One of the most common questions a financial advisor will be asked during their career is 'should I invest in property or a pension for retirement'. Therefore, I will now spend some time discussing the pensions vs property for retirement debate.

Investment growth

Capital growth

The primary way an investor will make money out of their investment is through capital growth. This is through buying an asset, i.e. a property or pension at a certain price and selling this asset at a higher price.

In simplistic terms, if an investor buys a property for £100,000 and sells this property for £200,000 there has been capital growth of £100,000 (sale price of £200,000 less cost price of £100,000).

The same process is applied to a pension, i.e. if total contributions equal £100,000 in total and the value of this pension increases to £200,000 at retirement then the investor has made a gain of £100,000.

The property market has consistently proven itself to be a successful investment over the long term and has enjoyed extraordinary capital growth over the years. House prices have comfortably beaten inflation by 3% per year since 1955 [19].

However, the UK stock market has grown by double that rate, beating inflation and achieving capital growth of 6% above inflation on average over the same time period, although these figures exclude rental and dividend income.

Rental income versus dividends

If you are investing in buy-to-let property, in addition to capital growth you will want to be able to get the highest rental yield possible to increase your overall return.

Rental yield is the return your property achieves through the rent you are able to charge your tenants. It is calculated by dividing the total yearly rental income by the amount you have invested in the property, for example a property that cost £100,000 that is receiving rental income of £6,000 gross per annum (£500 per month) has a rental yield of 6% (rental income of £6,000 divided by the cost of the property of £100,000). Please note that this figure is gross before any costs such as tax, insurance, repairs etc.

The equivalent to rental yield in the stock market world is dividend yield which measures how much a company pays out in dividends per year relative to its share price. For example, if a company paid out £5 in dividends per share and its shares currently cost £100, its dividend yield is 5%.

The most recent figures show that the average UK rental yield is currently 3.53% [20] and the average dividend yield as of the 31st of December 2020 in the FTSE 100 was 3.77% [21].

Please note that these dividend yield figures need to be taken into context in light of the current Covid-19 pandemic, as over half FTSE 100 companies either suspended (banks such as HSBC & Barclays) or reduced (BP and Shell) their dividend payments which has in turn reduced the overall dividend yield in the FTSE 100. This is further supported by the fact that the dividend yield in the FTSE 100 as at the 30th of June 2020 was 4.81% before certain large FTSE 100 companies reduced or suspending their dividend payments.

Please also note that both these rental and dividend yields are averages and will vary around the UK with certain areas generating higher and lower yields and certain FTSE 100 companies offering higher and lower dividend yields than others.

Therefore, in pure investments terms, pensions/investments look like a better investment than buy-to-let property investing for retirement based solely on total returns. However, there are other factors than need to be considered before being able to make an informed decision.

Taxation

Pensions are the one of the most (if not the most) tax efficient ways to save for retirement.

Taxation on the way in

One of the main benefits of a pension is its tax treatment. For example, for every £100 you want to contribute to a pension, the cost is only £80 to the individual with the Government making up the additional £20, this is called tax relief and it is the Government's way of incentivising you to save for your own retirement so that you will be less reliant on the Government to fund your retirement.

Please note that this is based on the individual being a basic rate tax payer, i.e. your total gross income for the tax year is less than £50,000.

It is even more tax efficient for a higher or additional rate tax payer. For a higher rate tax payer, i.e. total gross income for the tax year is above £50,000, the cost of a £100 contribution into your pension is only £60 and for an additional rate tax payer, i.e. total gross income for the tax year is £150,000 the cost of a £100 contribution is only £55.

This is where a pension comes into its own as there is no tax relief for a property purchase and usually any money being used to fund a property purchase comes from net, i.e. already taxed income.

Currently, any property purchase that isn't the investor's main residence will incur a stamp duty land tax charge of 3% if the purchase price is over £125,000. This obviously applies to buy-to-let properties (as the buy-to-let won't be the investor's main residence); therefore, a buy-to-let property purchase for £250,000 will incur a £2,500 tax charge. Please note that this is in addition to solicitor, estate agency fees etc

Taxation whilst owning pension/property

Once the pension has started there are also tax advantages, as investment returns that grow within the pension are free from capital gains tax which in turn allows the pension fund to grow quicker as less money is going to the tax man.

Any rent received from a buy-to-let property is taxable at the investor's marginal rate, i.e. the rate at which they pay tax. For example, if the investor is a basic rate tax payer the tax man will take 20% of any rental income received, and if the investor is a higher rate tax payer the tax man will take 40% of any rental income received. However, please note that property investors can deduct certain costs directly associated with the rental property from the rental income which can reduce the tax paid.

Taxation on the way out

Whenever the pension holder reaches 55 (although this age is increasing to 57 between 2026 and 2028) they are able to access their pension and usually the pension holder can withdraw the first 25% of the value of the pot tax free. The rest of the pension is then taxable at the tax payer's marginal rate.

Example

If a basic rate tax payer has reached 55 and has a pension fund worth £100,000, they could take the first £25,000 out tax free leaving them with a pension pot of £75,000.

If they took out the rest of the £75,000 pot as a lump sum then this £75,000 would be added on to their other sources of income for the tax year, as any taxable income taken from a pension pot is deemed to be earned income in the tax year it is taken out, which would take them into a higher tax band.

If the same individual had gross earnings of £30,000, a further £75,000 withdrawal from their pension would result in that individual having taxable income of £105,000 (£30,000 of earnings and £75,000 pension withdrawal). This results in a tax bill of £26,000* on the £75,000 pension withdrawal as the majority of this withdrawal will be taxed at 40%, resulting in the pension holder only receiving £49,000 net from their £75,000 withdrawal which is an effective tax rate of 34.67%!!!

*£20,000 @ 20% = £4,000 + £55,000 @ 40% = £22,000, therefore total tax liability = £26,000

If the same individual was retired, resulting in them having no taxable income (as they are now retired and have no earnings), they could take out £12,500 every year from their £75,000 pension until there is nothing left in their pension pot, fully utilizing their personal allowance of £12,500 every year, and incur no tax liability at all.

On the sale of a buy-to-let property, any profit is usually liable to capital gains tax (CGT), although purchase and sales costs are deductible. The CGT rates are 18% for basic rate tax payers and 28% for higher rate tax payers.

Therefore, a pension is a much more efficient retirement vehicle than a property based purely on tax as any investment into a pension receives tax relief on any contributions on the way into a pension, investments within a pension grow in a very tax efficient environment whilst they are in a pension and 25% of the pension can usually be taken out of a pension at retirement age tax free.

Whereas the purchase of a buy-to-let property doesn't receive tax relief on the initial investment. Any deposit being used to purchase a buy-to-let property is funded from taxed income. A 3% stamp duty tax charge is usually applied on the purchase price, any rental income received (minus any deductions) is usually taxed at the investor's marginal rate and capital gains tax is charged at 18% or 28% on any profit from the sale of a buy-to-let property

In addition, whenever a property is sold, the profit can't be spread over a number of tax years, whereas with a pension there is many more tax planning opportunities, as per above, and withdrawals can be spread across different tax years to take advantage and maximise personal allowances and different tax bands resulting in less tax being paid.

Furthermore, there have been a number of legislative changes to property investing in recent years such as the introduction of an additional 3% stamp duty land tax charge on the purchase of any 2nd properties, changes to the 10% wear and tear allowance rules for buy-to-lets, and a reduction in the amount of tax relief that can be deducted on buy-to-let mortgage payments – all of which have made property investing less attractive to prospective investors.

Inheritance tax/on-death considerations

When you die, your estate will be subject to inheritance tax (IHT), as covered in chapter 8, and this includes properties you own (including your main residence) and any investments, i.e. a share portfolio.

The current IHT threshold is £325,000 for a single person (£650,000 for a married couple) and if the total value of your estate, i.e. everything you own less anything you owe, is worth more than £325,000, your estate will pay 40% on the amount over the IHT threshold. So, for example if the total value of your estate is £500,000, then your estate will pay an inheritance tax bill of £70,000 (£500,000 less £325,000 = £175,000 x 40%).

However, pensions are usually exempt from IHT (although there are some restrictions) and they therefore will not form part of your estate for IHT purposes.

Generally, the rule is if you die before age 75, whatever is in your pension pot on death will be passed on to your chosen beneficiary/beneficiaries free of tax. If you die at the age of 75 or above, your pension will be passed on to your chosen beneficiary/ beneficiaries and they will pay tax at their marginal rate, i.e. if they are a basic rate payer they will pay tax at 20%.

If you have a potential IHT liability, e.g. the total value of your estate is more than £325,000 and you were using a combination of property income, investments and a pension to fund your retirement, you might be better to use up any IHT taxable assets, i.e. the investments and property first to reduce the value of your estate and in turn reduce or eliminate any IHT liability on death. Save your pension money until last.

Risk

The main risk of investing in property is that it won't rise in value over time and your rental income is outweighed by the costs of managing the property.

A range of regulatory and tax changes have made buy-to-let investing a much less lucrative and less attractive option especially for small-time landlords. It's worth crunching the numbers to work out if this option is still a worthwhile retirement vehicle.

You will also need to be prepared for void periods when the property is empty between tenancies and tenants who cause damage and/or don't pay their rent.

If you don't want to be a hands-on landlord and decide not to be involved in the day-to-day running of the property, you'll need to find and pay an agent who you trust to deal with your tenants and manage repairs or deal with any issues that arise.

In addition, whenever you are thinking about how to make money investing in property, you'll also need to plan your exit strategy, i.e. will you be able to sell your property and make a profit in the future? Where is it located, is it a nice area, will it attract reliable tenants?

Equally, there are risks to investing into a pension, the main one being whether you will get back less than you put in, although this is pretty unlikely given the length of time you will more than likely be invested. But, if your pension pot doesn't grow as expected, you could potentially run out of money in retirement.

Cost

When you invest into a pension, you can pay management fees on the funds you hold, transaction fees, platform fee and advice fees to your financial advisor. These regular fees can add up.

However, pensions have the advantage of giving you tax relief on your contributions which can mitigate the impact of fees, but you do have to pay income tax on anything you withdraw from your pension above the 25% tax free allowance.

With property, you pay larger one-off costs, mainly in the form of taxes although conveyancing or other legal fees, maintenance costs, agency or other management costs can also significantly eat into your returns.

You'll more than likely pay stamp duty land tax on the purchase of your property, income tax on your rental income and capital gains tax whenever you sell the property. After you die, the property (if not sold) will form part of your estate for inheritance tax purposes so it could be liable for inheritance tax.

Other considerations

In addition there are other factors that need to be considered before deciding on what is the best option.

Property can be very time consuming and requires a lot of effort. Finding tenants, dealing with letting agencies, arranging mortgages and re-mortgages, maintenance, repairs, decorations and insurance. Buying and selling is costly and also can be drawn out. If you have more than one property, it is like running a small business. A pension on the other hand is a lot less time consuming and any management of a pension is carried out by the fund manager (albeit for a fee).

Pensions do not have void periods. Void periods are periods where a rental property is without a tenant (although pensions allowed to hold commercial property could fall foul of void periods).

There is no guarantee that the property will always have tenants. If using rental income as income to help fund retirement, even short void periods will have a significant impact on returns.

Another important consideration to remember is that your pension provider will not contact the pension holder on a Saturday evening to advise that the boiler has broken down!!!

Viewing your home as your pension

Although the primary method of property investing is via buy-to-let investing, some individuals may view their home as their pension or as another way to generate money to help fund their retirement alongside their pension.

As we have already mentioned, property prices have soared over the years and the chances are if you bought your house over 15 – 20 years ago, the value of your home will be more than you paid for it.

Therefore, an option is to sell or downsize your home and live off the proceeds. For example, if you bought your home for £50,000 and sold it for £200,000 this would generate you a nice profit of £150,000 which in turn could help fund your retirement.

However, although downsizing may make financial sense, other factors may be of equal importance such as being comfortable with leaving friends and memories behind; also, getting used to the fact that you will more than likely be moving into a smaller home. In this respect it may be as much of an emotional decision as it is a financial one.

Another option is equity release, which involves using the equity or value of your home to provide you with a lump sum now with the equity release provider recouping its money by selling your home after you die.

However, equity release can be expensive and the interest rates on this type of borrowing can be very high. As an option it should be handled carefully as although it may be suitable for some people, it should only usually be considered after all other options have been considered, and requires professional, impartial advice.

Pros and cons of investing in property for retirement

Pros of investing in property

- You own a real asset

- Property values tend to increase over time; therefore, you can benefit from capital growth

- You also will benefit from rental income which should in turn increase your overall profit

- You can use gearing – borrowing money from a bank to purchase a property or multiple properties and use the rental income received from your tenant/s to pay this off over a period of time. In theory, you will have a mortgage-free property/properties which cost you nothing other than the initial deposit.

Cons of investing in property

- You pay capital gains on property when you sell, income tax on your rental income and inheritance tax when you die.

- Property is an illiquid asset so your money is tied up for a long time.

- You may not be able to sell your property whenever you want to and/or you may then have to accept a price you are not happy with.

- You may pay more tax now as a buy-to-let landlord because, for example, you can no longer claim tax relief on mortgage interest payments.

- You may have to pay stamp duty when you buy a property.

- Costs can be high, such as repairs, maintenance, legal fees, surveyor fees, agent fees, insurance and you could lose money from non-paying tenants or void periods.

- You can spend a lot of time and effort managing a property yourself and you have legal responsibilities as a landlord.

Pros and cons of investing into a pension for retirement

Pros of a pension

- You get free money from the Government in the form of tax relief on your contributions.

- If you are in employment, your employer has to pay into your workplace pension, which is in effect 'free' money.

- Your money is usually invested in a diversified portfolio of assets (including property if you like), spreading your risk.

- If you start saving early, the power of compound interest means that your pot could grow significantly.

- You can in theory set up and forget your pension (although it's better to review on a regular basis) whereas a property is much more hands-on.

- Your pension is protected if the FCA regulated provider goes bust.

- Contributions are flexible and you can start small.

- You can time/plan withdrawals to reduce your tax bill, as part of tax planning.

Cons of a pension

- Your money is locked away in a private pension until age 55 (this is due to increase to age 57 in 2028).

- Your pension can fall as well as rise, i.e. there is no guarantee in investment performance; therefore, you could, in theory, run out of money in retirement.

- You have to pay investment fees and charges on your pension.

- You will more than likely pay income tax on anything you withdraw above the 25% tax free lump sum.

- Various scandals have tarnished consumer trust in the pensions industry.

Example

To give us a better idea to see if investing in property is better investment than a pension, let's look at a real-life example. Please note that this example is based on 2020/21 UK tax rates and tax bands.

John has built up a pension pot of £300,000 and is thinking about buying a property he likes to help fund his eventual retirement. He thinks that buying this property and renting it out might provide better returns than leaving the money in his pension. He cashes in his whole pension to buy the property.

John earns £30,000 gross per annum. His pension withdrawal will result in a loss of his personal allowance* and an additional tax bill of £96,250.**

He will have a tax bill of £99,750 in total for the year including his earnings, compared to a £3,500 tax bill – based on his £30,000 gross earnings – without taking the pension withdrawal.

*The personal allowance is reduced by £1 for every £2 earned over £100,000, and as the pension withdrawal will result in John 'earning over £125,000 in the year of withdrawal he will lose his personal allowance in full.

**The first 25%, i.e. £75,000 of the pension would be tax free. John has £20,000 of his basic rate band left (basic rate threshold of £50,000 less earnings of £30,000) – therefore £20,000 at 20% = £4,000; the next £100,000 (higher rate threshold of £150,000 less basic rate threshold of £50,000) would be taxed at 40% – therefore £100,000 x 40% = £40,000, and finally the residual £105,000 would be taxed at the additional rate of 45% – therefore £105,000 x 45% = £47,250. Finally, as John loses his personal allowance this will result in an additional £12,500 being taxed at 40%; therefore £12,500 x 40% = £5,000.

In reality, the withdrawal is likely to be subject to emergency month 1 tax (also known as emergency tax) resulting in an initial tax bill of £99,524. He would of course be able to claim back any overpaid tax from HMRC.

For the purposes of this example, we will assume John isn't subject to the emergency tax code. As a result there would be £203,750 (£300,000 less tax bill of £96,250) left in John's pension to purchase the property.

Out of this amount, a number of costs will need to be taken into account. These may include:

- £7,500*** Stamp Duty Land Tax

- £1,375 solicitor/survey fees (estimated)

- £2,000 white goods/furniture costs (assuming that John is renting the property out furnished/part furnished). Even unfurnished properties usually provide certain white goods such as a cooker, washing machine etc as unfurnished properties without basic amenities can be difficult to let.

*** *The first £125,000 is taxed at 3% equalling £3,750 and the next £75,000 is taxed at 5% equalling another £3,750. Total is therefore £7,500.*

So, with estimated costs of £10,875, John only has £192,875 of the original pot left (£300,000 less £96,250 less £10,875) to buy the property.

Unfortunately, the property John likes costs £200,000. As such, despite starting off with a pension of £300,000, John needs to use £7,125 of his savings to fund the property purchase.

In addition, John has decided to rent out his property via a letting agent as he doesn't want the hassle of advertising the property, interviewing/ vetting potential tenants, arranging tenancy agreements, collecting rent, completing inspections etc.

The selected agency charges 10% of the gross rental income for their services but they have managed to find a tenant prepared to rent the property for £1,000 per month. Fortunately, the tenant also takes care of the property so he incurs no costs in replacing damaged fixtures and fittings.

Any rental income is taxable, therefore John has to pay tax on the rental amount, after paying the letting agent fee, so his annual income from the property will be;

£1,000 x 12 = £12,000 – 10% = £10,800 – 20% (basic rate tax) = £8,640 (this may be higher in the initial period as the pension withdrawal resulted in emergency tax being applied.).

This may seem okay to John; however, there are a number of issues that he has to consider.

As a net income, relative to his original pension fund of £300,000 and the additional £7,125, the net yield from the rent is actually only 2.81%**** per annum which is perhaps not as attractive as John initially thought. He wonders how this compares with the yield his pension would have produced had he left the funds within his pension.

*****£8,640/£307,125 = 2.81%*

Please note that a net average annual return of 4.5 – 5% would be typical of a medium risk pension fund, although this is not guaranteed.

Other potential issues to consider

- If John was to become a higher rate tax payer, he would receive a net return of £6,480 (£10,800 – 40% = £6,480), which would reduce his net income yield relative to his original pension fund to **2.11%****

*****£6,480/307,125 x 100 = 2.11%*

- Capital gains tax of 18% or 28% will usually be paid on any gain/profit on the property whenever it is eventually sold. For example, if the property is sold for £300,000, there will be a gain of £100,000 (sales proceeds of £300,000 less purchase price of £200,000) which will result in a considerable capital gains tax liability.

- On John's death inheritance tax could be payable on the property (with a pension this is unlikely as pensions don't usually form part of the estate for inheritance tax purposes).

- There is no guarantee that the property will always have tenants and even a short void period would have a significant impact on the return. For example, one void month each year would reduce the above yield to below **2.58%******* (based on a basic rate tax payer), and given that John is using the rent to fund his retirement, void periods could have a significant impact on his standard of living.

***** *£1,000 x 11 = £11,100 – 10% = £9,900 – 20% (basic rate tax) =*
£7,920/307,125 = 2.58%

- There could be maintenance and/or repair costs (tenants don't always look after the property the way the landlord wants them to). Large repairs like a roof replacement or replacing a boiler can be costly and this will again have an impact on the yield.

- If the tenants have problems and can't get in touch with the letting agent, John may start to receive phone calls from them.

- The value of the property or the rental income may fall.

- Unpaid rent may be unrecoverable, and this may in turn result in litigation costs.

- Litigation (and associated costs) may be required to remove a tenant who won't abide by the terms and conditions of their lease.

- There is also a potential issue regarding John's ability to access money tied up in his property, especially in a downward market or with a sitting tenant. Given John's property was to fund his retirement, this may become a major issue.

- Investing all his pension funds in property may result in a lack of diversification. Putting all your eggs in the one basket can be a very high-risk strategy.

On the Upside

- The property may increase in value and this would increase John's overall return whenever he sells it. However, please note that this increase in value would only be realised on sale and any gain would be potentially liable to capital gains tax.

- John may get a long-term tenant who pays the rent on time and looks after the property, and as a result the rental yield, property prices and capital gains tax may be the only issues John needs to consider.

Of course, if John is adamant that property is his preferred investment of choice, another potential option is investing indirectly in property with his pension via a well-diversified multi-asset pension fund which invests part of the overall pot in property funds.

In conclusion, from a purely financial point of view, using a pension is more than likely a better option than property investment for retirement purposes, mainly due to the tax advantages associated with a pension (especially for a higher rate tax payer). In addition, property investment is much more time consuming and more hassle than owning a pension.

However, this isn't to say that property investment isn't a viable option to help fund your retirement. There are plenty of people who like the idea of borrowing funds to help build a considerable property portfolio, and other people who like the fact that a property is tangible unlike a pension. For people who are familiar with and who work within the property industry, i.e. builders, tradesmen, professional buy-to-let investors etc, they understand the property business and may be more comfortable with a buy-to-let property than a pension.

Both have their advantages and disadvantages and what is right for you will depend on your own individual circumstances and how comfortable you are with the risks involved. There is no reason pensions and property can't compliment each other as part of a diverse retirement strategy.

Pension versus ISA

Although, property investment is a very common and popular method for many individuals for retirement planning, a pension and also an individual savings account (more commonly known as an ISA) offer more and better tax benefits and would both be more tax efficient vehicles for retirement.

Both pensions and ISAs have their particular advantages and tax breaks and allow you to grow a nest egg for your retirement in a tax efficient manner. There are big differences in the way that they are taxed and we will look at this now.

We have already covered the tax treatment of a pension. However, in order to compare a pension and an ISA, it would do no harm to cover this again.

In general, there are three stages at which the taxman can take a slice of your money. The first is before the money is put into a savings pot. The second is whilst the money is in the pot and the third is when the money is withdrawn from the pot.

Stage 1 – Paying money in

A major benefit of a pension over almost every other savings vehicle is that when you pay money into a pension, you get an income tax refund (better known as 'tax relief') on any contributions. In other words, the taxman helps out by refunding some of the tax which you've already paid, either directly into your pension or as a rebate following your tax return.

For example, if you make a £80 contribution into a pension, the Government will add £20, making your gross contribution £100

Furthermore, higher rate (40%) and additional rate (45%) taxpayers can claim a further £20 and £25 tax rebate respectively via their tax return.

Hence, a £100 gross contribution into a pension costs a basic rate tax payer £80, a higher rate payer £60 and an additional rate payer £55!

With an employer/workplace pension, your pension contributions are usually deducted straight from your salary every month. Rather than receiving an income tax refund, you won't pay any tax on your contribution which means that you will receive your tax relief straight away (i.e. if you make a monthly contribution of £100 and earn £2,000 gross per month, this £100 contribution will be deducted from your gross salary straight into your pension and as a result you will only pay tax on the remaining £1,900 of your wages).

Consequently, you will pay less tax because less of your wages are being taxed. If you didn't make this £100 contribution to your pension, this £100 would have been taxed at 20% if you were a basic rate, and 40% and 45% for higher and additional payers.

The maximum amount you can normally save into a pension annually and receive tax relief on is currently 100% of your salary, up to a maximum of £40,000.

Please note that even if you don't pay tax at all, you can currently still claim tax relief on a certain level of contribution. In fact, you can contribute up to £2,880 per tax year into a personal pension and the taxman will add up to £720, making your gross contribution £3,600.

With an ISA, you don't get a tax refund whenever you pay money in, so an £80 contribution will remain £80 in total.

The maximum amount you can save into an ISA is currently £20,000 per individual for the 2020/21 tax year.

Stage 2 – Whilst the money is invested

Pensions and ISAs are very similar in their tax treatment of any money invested in each. In both cases any investment gains are largely exempt from any tax, so the position would be tax neutral at this stage.

Stage 3 – Withdrawing money

When you come to take your money out, it is largely a reversal of the position at the first stage. Any withdrawals from an ISA are not taxed but any withdrawals from a pension are subject to tax at the individual's marginal rate, i.e. if the individual is a basic rate tax payer any withdrawals will be taxed at 20%.

However, the first 25% of the value of a pension can usually be taken tax free. Therefore, based on a pension pot of £100,000, the first £25,000 can be taken tax free and the residual £75,000 will be taxed at the individual's marginal rate.

As you can see, at first sight there is not a lot to choose between a pension and an ISA as far as tax relief is concerned. Pensions seem to be more tax efficient when paying money in whereas ISAs are more so when withdrawing.

However, it's not as simple at that. Let's look at an example, for both basic and higher rate payers, which can hopefully shed a bit more light on which vehicle is the better option.

Please note that the following example assumes that the individual makes an initial investment of £20,000 (as per the maximum current ISA contribution limit) and makes a net return of 4% per annum after charges. It is also assumed that the whole fund is taken as a lump sum after 10 years of investment.

Investment Wrapper	Initial Investment	Value after 10 years	Tax-Free Cash	Taxable Lump sum (net of tax)	Total Net Return
ISA – Regardless of tax band	£20,000	£29,605	-	-	£29,605
Pension – Basic rate taxpayer	£25,000*	£37,006	£9,251	£22,203	£31,454
Pension - Higher rate taxpayer at start and basic rate tax payer after 10 years	£30,000**	£44,407	£11,101	£26,644	£37,745

*Net contribution of £20,000 plus tax relief at the basic rate of £5,000

**Net contribution of £20,000 plus tax relief at the basic rate of £5000. Client also reclaims £5000 higher rate tax relief.

The table above illustrates that when you compare the three different scenarios, the pension will deliver the highest post tax/net return.

There are other scenarios that you could consider, including that an individual is a basic rate tax payer at the outset and a higher rate tax payer at retirement or at withdrawal stage. This could be the case if a sizable lump sum withdrawal is taken from the pension whilst the individual is still working full time, which may bring them into a higher rate tax band (as any pension withdrawal over and above the 25% tax free amount is deemed taxable income for income tax purposes). In this scenario an ISA would be much more tax efficient and would most likely be the preferred option. Even borrowing would be a better option in this scenario.

However, most individuals will likely pay the same or a lower tax rate at retirement as they will most likely be earning less in retirement than what they were earning during their career, therefore the two scenarios in the table are the two most common scenarios likely to happen.

On pure tax grounds, due to the tax relief on the contributions, it is difficult to beat a pension. This is particularly the case for someone who is a higher rate taxpayer when making the pension contribution but a basic rate taxpayer whenever they are taking the benefits.

More money is invested which means that the pension may benefit from growth on the tax relief and it is invested in a tax efficient fund. In addition, whenever the benefits are taken, 25% of the fund value is normally available as tax free cash.

Other considerations

As previously illustrated, the tax wrapper is an important part in determining the overall investment return. However, tax is not the only consideration.

Flexibility

You can only usually access your pension money when you reach 55 and this age is due to increase to 57 from 2028. When you are 55, you have a number of options. You can take up to 25% as a tax-free lump sum, you can leave your money invested and take cash lump sums out whenever you need them (via drawdown), or you can use your pension to purchase a guaranteed income for the rest of your life (via an annuity).

Whereas with an ISA you can access your money whenever you want – although if you are investing in a stocks and shares ISA, an investment term of at least five years is highly recommended.

Or, you can split money between a cash ISA and a stocks and shares ISA and move the money whenever you want.

Prior to April 2016, if an individual needed to access money from their ISA, the money could not be replaced unless there was some of the annual limit remaining. Since the 6th of April 2016 an investor can replace money they have withdrawn earlier in a tax year. Please note, though, that not all ISA providers will offer this flexibility.

Although an ISA offers more flexibility than a pension in terms of having access to your money, the primary purpose of your pension is to fund your retirement. As such, not having access to your pension until aged 55 may actually be a positive thing as it removes any temptation to access your retirement pot early!

Inheritance/legacy

A big benefit of a personal pension is that it doesn't usually form part of your estate in the event of your death, so your pension isn't included in your estate for inheritance tax purposes.

Although the primary purpose of your pension is to provide you with an income in retirement, a secondary benefit is that it can be a very effective vehicle for inheritance tax purposes.

For example, if the value of your estate is, say, £1 million, and is made up of your main residence, a couple of buy-to-let properties and some savings and investments (remember any pensions aren't included in the value of your estate for inheritance tax purposes), the best option here might be to use your savings and investments (rather than your pension) to fund your retirement as this will help reduce the value of your estate and in turn reduce or potentially eliminate any potential inheritance tax liability in the event of your death.

If you used your pension to fund your retirement, the value of your savings and investments would continue to grow which would in turn increase the value of your estate and also your inheritance tax bill.

In addition, another benefit of a pension is that if you pass away before aged 75, the value of your pension is passed on to your beneficiaries tax free.

If you pass away after the age of 75, your beneficiaries will have to pay tax at their marginal rate, i.e. if they are a basic rate taxpayer they will pay 20% tax on any withdrawals.

The rationale behind this is that it is likely that you will have more than likely started to use your pension by age 75 which should drive down its value and in turn reduce any potential income tax liability for your beneficiaries.

In contrast, any ISA savings are counted as part of your estate, so they'll be added to your other savings and assets when you die and your beneficiaries may in turn have to pay inheritance tax.

Inheritance tax is due on estates over £325,000 and is charged at 40%. However, this doesn't apply if you're passing your money onto your spouse or civil partner.

Previously, your ISA always lost its tax-free status when it was inherited, but since April 2015, in the event of death, your ISA can be passed on tax free to your spouse or civil partner with its benefits being retained, giving your partner a temporary additional allowance.

Different Life Stages

As previously discussed, a pension is the most suitable retirement vehicle for almost all circumstance due mainly to its tax advantages and also its inheritance/legacy benefits.

Early Career: Aged 25–45

However as previously discussed, the one area in which an ISA is more attractive than a pension is accessibility.

Your pension savings are, in most cases, not accessible until age 55, and for younger savers who are likely to need access before this age or as an emergency or medium-term fund, an ISA becomes a more suitable option.

If you have any uncertainties about when you may need to access your money or you need access over the short to medium term, your best bet would be an ISA.

Mid Late Career: Age 45–55

In the latter stages of your working life, the decision becomes more straightforward.

In most cases, a pension should be the preferred option, provided that you have some accessible savings for emergency purposes.

You are unlikely to retire at 55 and probably won't want to draw from your pension pot while you are still working, but it's not too long to wait before you can access your pension and the tax benefits are superior with a pension.

If you are a higher rate taxpayer, the benefits are particularly appealing, especially if, like most people, you will become a basic rate tax payer in retirement.

Perhaps the only reason you should pick an ISA over a pension at this stage is if your pension is at risk of breaching annual allowance or lifetime limits. Therefore, if you have funded your pension as much as you are allowed to, you should think of using an ISA to fund your retirement.

Pre-retirement and retirement: 55 Onwards

For most individuals, your state pension will form a considerable part of your retirement income, especially married couples.

The full state pension is currently £9,110 per annum and for a married couple who are both entitled to the full state pension this will generate £18,220 (£9,110 x 2) which is a nice start to your retirement.

However, if you retire before the state pension age, currently 66, you will need to potentially use other sources of income as well as your pension pot. You will need to keep in mind that your retirement could last maybe another 40 years, so you will need to plan carefully how much you can afford to draw from your pot.

Often the first port of call is the 25% tax-free element of your pension, as there are no tax implications of taking this.

Importantly, if you do choose this option and then decide to start using the residual 75% of your pension (which is taxable), you will need to be careful that any subsequent withdrawals don't bring you into a higher rate tax band.

There is an argument for withdrawing income from an ISA at this time as you won't pay tax on any withdrawals and in addition you can leave your pension to grow for longer.

In this situation, pensions and ISAs really complement each other, so a combination can work well. As any withdrawals from ISAs are tax free, it makes sense to keep any pension income under the tax threshold and use your ISA to help fund your retirement while avoiding the higher rate tax bracket (currently at £50,000).

In addition, this will also help reduce/eliminate any potential inheritance tax liability by reducing the value of your estate.

Pros and cons of Pension versus ISA

Pension – Advantages

- The fund is locked away: the earliest you can access it is age 55 (57 from 2028).

- You get tax relief on contributions at your marginal rate, so more beneficial to higher rate taxpayers.

- Generally you can potentially save more each year in a pension (up to £40,000) than an ISA (£20,000).

- Pensions do not usually count for inheritance tax purposes.

- Pensions are not usually taken into account should you ever need means-tested benefits

Pension – Disadvantages

- The fund is locked away until you're 55 (57 from 2028).

- Apart from the 25% tax free lump sum, the benefits are taxable.

ISA – Advantages

- Although there are no tax breaks on the way in – i.e. contributions – any withdrawals are tax free.

- You can access the money at any time.

- ISAs can be inherited (between spouses and civil partners) without penalty.

- They do not need to be declared on your tax return.

ISAs – Disadvantages

- You can freely access the money and it can be tempting to dip in. You have to be very disciplined!

- You are limited in the amount you can put away each year (currently £20,000).

- They will count as savings should you need to resort to means-tested benefits.

Conclusion

In summary, although an ISA may offer more flexibility than a pension, especially for younger people, the tax advantages of a pension would, in most circumstances, make it the preferred retirement planning option for most individuals, especially those who are higher and additional rate tax payers during their working lives and basic rate tax payers during retirement.

A pension would also be the preferred option for any workers who have access to a workplace pension due to the tax benefits of employee contributions and also because the employer must contribute to this pension and any employer contributions would be deemed as 'free' money.

Finally, a pension is also an attractive tax wrapper from an inheritance tax perspective, as an Isa will form part of an investor's estate on death, whereas a pension won't usually form part of the deceased estate.

Therefore, the argument to use a pension over any other investment vehicle for retirement planning purposes is fairly compelling.

Chapter 5

Options at retirement – part 1

"Money does not guarantee success." Jose Mourinho

Seven key questions you need to answer before retiring.

Deciding to retire and how best to access your pension pots can be very stressful. The main reasons for this stress tend to be a mixture of confusion, fear of making the wrong decisions, overwhelmed with choices and perhaps horror stories you have read in the financial press.

When faced with these worries, some retirees also have the stress of deciding whether or not they need financial advice, and if so how they choose the right advisor.

In this chapter, we have put together seven key questions that we believe are crucial to answer before deciding how best to use your pensions, savings and investments at retirement.

Understanding the answers to these questions is vital before explaining the financial options that are open to you upon retirement. By answering these questions, they can help you on your own or through the services of a financial planner decide which of the many options at retirement is best for you.

1. How much income will you need?

As this chapter focuses on those decisions at the point of retirement, we explore in more depth your likely projected expenditure. The closer you get to retirement, the easier it is to be more detailed in your likely expenses.

There are three stages to retirement. For clients getting advice at retirement, it's for this reason we prefer a projected expenses list that asks not only what your expenses are today, but also how you estimate these may change as you get older.

1. Early retirement.
2. Late retirement.
3. Retirement with care.

Early retirement

Your early retirement years start when you leave your regular full-time work, or sell a business, usually anywhere between your fifties and late sixties. This does not necessarily mean you completely stop work. For some it's a reduction to part-time working within their existing job or for others a change of career.

I can't help noticing the older age demographic of employees in B&Q when I am in their store. This is an excellent example of many retirees passing on a lifetime of experience whilst continuing to earn income in a less stressful environment.

Whether it's a change of career or a reduction in working hours there are benefits to employment at this stage. The obvious one being extra income but perhaps also for our mental health as we "stay in touch with society". There is no doubt working gives us a sense of purpose and identity that can be lost when some retire fully.

In a 2019 report by the Office of National Statistics it showed that the number of over-65's continuing to work has doubled in the past 20 years. [22]

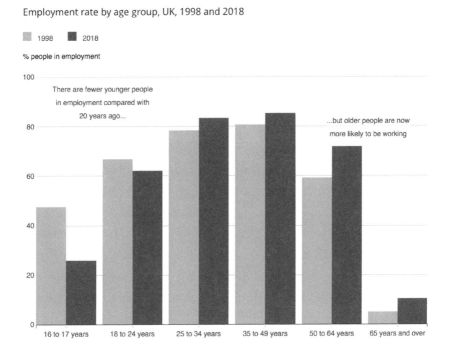

Employment rate by age group, UK, 1998 and 2018

During this time retirees maintain a more active lifestyle which requires a higher level of income than late retirement. I regularly see clients taking holidays, and indeed some even purchase a holiday home either in the UK or abroad. Some retirees wisely take 'long haul holidays' at this time as they feel they won't have the appetite for travelling longer distances as they age.

Late retirement

Later retirement years are generally in your seventies and eighties. For those who continued to earn in the early stage of retirement, employment or business income may now have stopped, and they are largely reliant upon pension income and savings.

Inevitably there may be changes in what activities you can and cannot do as medical issues may arise during these years. You may now be reassessing if your home remains manageable and in the right location. Convenient access to shops, medical centres and family start to come into your thinking.

Holidays start to be reduced both in frequency and in distance from home. This is not just driven by health and mobility, but the cost of travel insurance, which increases. Some household bills may increase as more time is spent in the home, whilst other expenses can reduce as a result of being less actively sociable.

Retirement with care

As you reach your late eighties and your nineties, medical and other care needs may dictate what you do and where you live.

Should your own income not cover the costs your capital, in some cases your home may need to be used to fund care home fees. The LaingBuisson Care of Older People Report 2019 estimates the cost of residential care in Northern Ireland to be £534 per week and Nursing Care to be £691 per week. These costs increase for conditions such as Dementia. [23]

For those in a relationship

The dynamic of how couples jointly manage household income and expenditure tends to vary. We often see examples where one account is shared for both money in and out of the household. Other clients find this idea uncomfortable with each partner holding their own account individually. Bills can then be paid for either from a joint account or by being shared out in an agreed manner.

Our view is that no matter how you manage household finances its vital that both parties record income & expenditure when planning for your retirement income. Sadly, at some point one in the relationship will pass away and allowances need to be made for the impact this will have financially. This is an important point often overlooked when deciding how best to use pensions and investments at retirement.

Example

Ben & Pam have a combined household income of £2500 per month. This is made up of Ben's state pension of £700 per month and an annuity of £1200 per month from his pension. Pam has a small state pension of £600 per month. Ben and Pam spend all their income each month and have a comfortable lifestyle.

Ben suddenly passes away and as Ben choose an annuity from his pension without any spouse pension or guarantees, this £1200 income payment will cease. On Ben's death this leaves Pam with only her state pension of £600 per month. Although the household bills will fall, they will still now be well above her income causing Pam financial difficulty.

Doing the maths

If you are someone who has always had a personal budget, this should be straightforward, and you simply need to think about how your expenditure may change once you retire – over the three phases of retirement.

Many people operate on autopilot when budgeting during their working life. They get used to an income and know more or less what they can afford to do on that budget without thinking about it in great detail, but everyone must understand things can change in retirement.

Matching up the normal household bills such as phone, electric and rates is straightforward. For those who don't know these figures, a glance through a recent bank statement will retrieve this information as they are normally paid via direct debit.

The biggest issue when trying to understand your expenditure is figuring out your irregular and discretionary expenditure. These are the items that are not direct debits, but may still be something you have to spend money on, if not each month then still regularly.

Example

Julie has gone through her bank statement and found the following direct debits

Electric £80
Rates £60
Telephone & Internet £60
Sky TV £55
Mobile Phone £30
Car Payment £200
Savings to Pension £100
Car Insurance £50

Total – £635

Julie earns £1600 per month and she finds at the end of the month she does not have any money left. She can't figure out where the rest of her income is being spent.

She starts to think about what else she spends money on regularly but is not a direct debit. She remembers two expenses:

Petrol £100
Food shopping £250

New Total £985

This still leaves £615 per month of income that she can't account for. Where is Julie regularly spending the other £615 per month of her salary?

Irregular expenses

Some expenses we incur regularly and frequently but are not direct debits and not paid on a monthly basis. Examples of these include birthday and Christmas presents, clothes, prescriptions, car fuel and maintenance.

Discretionary expenditure

These are costs you incur through your own lifestyle choices. Examples include takeaway drinks and snacks and eating out, day trips and holidays, cinema and theatre trips.

Understanding your spending habits when it comes to irregular and discretionary expenses is more difficult and does take thought.

It is worth mentioning that the definition of discretionary and fixed expenditure differs significantly from person to person. For example, some would consider golf fees essential and for others this would be discretionary.

Some tips

- start living on your retirement income six months before you retire. This gives you time to adjust your projected expenditure and ensure it's a more accurate reflection of how you spend your income.

- I think it best that all expenses are ultimately broken down to a monthly cost. For example, if you spend £360 at Christmas time on presents, allocate £30 per month as a cost. This will not only help budgeting, but also be easier to help you control your spending in retirement.

- keep track of your expenditure by means of a spending diary. Record everything you spend over a period of say one month so you can see what you are spending on, how much it is and crucially have you included it accurately in your own budgeting.

In the age of digital innovation there are a growing number of online and phone apps that help you draw up a budget planner based on your current spending. www.thisismoney.co.uk wrote an article in May 2020 highlighting their five best money management apps as [24]:

1. Cleo
2. Plum
3. Emma
4. Moneyhub
5. Snoop

Some of these apps can be automated to some degree if you allow the app to link directly to your bank account, credit card and other financial accounts.

If you prefer, there are online budget templates where you simply enter your own figures. For example, you could use the Money and Pensions Service budget planner as well as dedicated tools to see whether you have a budget shortfall in retirement.

How your expenditure can change

1. **What extra outgoings will you have?**

If you spend more time at home once you retire utility bills can increase. You might find you would like to spend more on outgoings such as hobbies and holidays.

2. **What are possible reductions in your spending?**

    Once you stop working there will be expenses that you no longer have. These could include costs of travelling to and from work, meals out, business clothes and other work-related incidentals such as staff nights out, staff collections and entertainment.

    Other costs, such as National Insurance contributions, cease once you reach state pension age, and unless you chose to invest in a private plan your pension contributions also stop.

    Your children may no longer be financially dependent on you and your mortgage could now be paid off.

    If some of your expenses continue for several months into your early retirement, capital can be set aside to cover these rather than including them in your expenses. For example, if your mortgage is £500 per month but expires six months after you retire, £6000 of capital could be used to cover this rather than include this as an expense.

3. **How might your expenditure change as you move into later retirement?**

    As mentioned, your lifestyle could well alter as you age. Try to quantify specifically what expenses will change and by how much. Perhaps your holiday costs will reduce but the household heating bill will increase as you spend more time at home?

4. **For those in a relationship, what expenditure would continue in the event of the first death?**

Not all expenses are automatically halved in the event of death, a good example is your household rates bill which does not change in the event of the first death within a relationship. However, some costs will reduce, such as your food bill. Try to quantify the exact total of the likely expenditure needs your partner may still have upon your death.

Final thoughts

The intention is to start thinking about the way your financial affairs might change when you retire and then pass through these three stages of retirement. Everyone has different circumstances and you need to pause and think about your own situation.

It is important to check, once you retire, what your tax code is because you may well move to a lower tax bracket and HMRC should be contacted if this is the case.

Remember, even though you have retired, if your income is above the personal allowance you still need to pay income tax.

Example

John has completed a full budget planner and established he needs £20,000 of income in retirement.

If John's pension income was £20,000, he would not have enough income to meet his needs due to income tax deduction.

Total Income £20,000.

Personal allowance is £12,500.

Taxable Income £7,500 x 20% income tax = £1,500.

Therefore, after income tax John's income would only be £18,500.

For John to have £20,000 net income after tax, he requires gross income of £21,875.

If you follow the suggestions that we have given you, adjusted as necessary to your own personal needs, you should have better control of your affairs. Don't forget the personal budget is not a precise science, you must be flexible and prepared to carry out adjustments as you go along. If things seem too complex you might need to engage the services of a financial advisor.

2. What other expenditure are you likely to have?

So far, we have considered your likely monthly expenditure in retirement. However, throughout our lifetime we will have incurred additional expenses that perhaps we have not planned for. Not every potential cost can be included in your budget planner as some expenses are simply a one off.

It's important we consider what other expenses we could have in retirement and how much they may cost. Failing to plan for these could result in using investment or pension pots allocated to support your monthly income. Spending money allocated to support your income on one-off expenses will reduce your monthly income. This will in turn mean a forced reduction in your lifestyle, which is not always possible.

From dealing with many clients over the years I have listed the main expenditure needs I have seen regularly. This is by no means an exhaustive list:

- **Bridging payments**

  I regularly meet clients who are needing or wanting to retire early. The state pension income forms a significant part of most retiree's income. Should retirement not be affordable without the state pension income, capital can be set aside to replace the state pension income until state pension age is reached.

Example

Max is age 60, and due to poor health he needs to retire now. His company pension is £1,200 per month after tax. Max needs £1,800 per month to live comfortably. His state pension will start in seven years time at age 67. Upon receiving his state pension he will have more income than he needs. Until age 67 he sets aside capital to cover this shortfall.

His shortfall is £600 per month; this equals £7200 per year. Over seven years this equals £50,400. He simply uses £600 per month of his savings pot over the seven years until his state pension begins.

- **Emergency funds**

We can't account for every expense in life that may come along. For this reason, it's important to set aside savings for the proverbial 'rainy day'. I have seen lots of suggestions about how much this needs to be. Quite often a multiple of your income is suggested such as six months income. If your salary is £2,000 per month then this means an emergency fund of £12,000.

In my opinion the amount of our emergency fund is a personal decision. It's based on your lifestyle and importantly how much you need to allocate that makes you feel comfortable. I have found significant variations in the amount of cash that clients feel they need to hold. Take some time to consider what emergencies could come up in your life and how much these would cost before deciding on a figure.

- **Debt repayment**

Sometimes when we reach retirement, we will still have outstanding debts such as a balance on the mortgage. It could be that retirement is unaffordable when the outstanding monthly mortgage cost is included in the monthly expenses. Should this be the case and the retiree holds the additional capital, this can then be used to repay the debt, removing it as a monthly expense.

- **Changing of a car**

A large percentage of us don't like car payments and therefore prefer to own a vehicle outright. For this reason, some retirees don't have this as a monthly cost. If this is the case, it's unlikely for someone retiring that the car won't need to be changed in the future, perhaps several times in their lifetime. For those in this category, an estimate of the likely costs of upgrading their car is important to consider.

- **Holidays**

Not everyone takes a holiday frequently. For some it may be a cost perhaps only once or twice in retirement. However, for those who consider themselves frequent travellers, a holiday budget will obviously depend on where and for how long.

- **Children's or other family members' weddings**

In the UK Wedding Report by Bridebook 2020, the average cost of a wedding in the UK was £20,731 [25]. It's an expensive event and many of us do like to help with the costs of the big day for our loved ones.

- **Gifts to help family buy property**

In 2019 Legal and General produced a report entitled 'The Bank of Mum and Dad' [26]. It makes excellent reading. The BOMAD, as it's known, is the 11th largest mortgage lender in the UK, contributing £6.3 billion in funding. Interestingly, 59% of the money was gifted outright.

- **University fees**

As I write, this is a sensitive topic. The current Covid-19 pandemic means a lot of students are trapped paying for face-to-face tuition along with rental fees on student accommodation. This is controversial as many are doing video tutorials at home in their bedroom!

University fees were first introduced here in the UK in 1998 when Tony Blair was the Prime Minister. However, as a result of the new devolved national administrations for Scotland, Wales and Northern Ireland, there are now different arrangements for tuition fees in each of the nations. In addition, accommodation can be another significant cost if the student can't stay at home.

Whilst it can be expensive, student loans are very popular in recent years to support these costs.

- **Gifts to family**

I am sure many parents would agree financially supporting your children rarely ends when they turn 18. Over the years I have regularly seen parents help their children who are struggling financially. By the same token I think it's fair to say that giving away too much money to your family can impact their ability to understand its true value. It's important to strike the balance between supporting your family and allowing them to develop the appreciation that comes with the hard work of earning something for themselves.

- **Buying a holiday home**

The Resolution Foundation Report in April 2018 [27] confirms that around 5.2 million people in the UK own second homes. This is around 10% of the population. With the recent Covid-19 pandemic this shows no signs of slowing down. I have met many clients who have owned properties locally as well as in Spain, Italy and France to name but a few. In my experience those who buy a property that's easy to travel to and from get the best value from their purchase.

Secondary to this, I think it's important to buy in a location you are sure you want to continually visit and perhaps spend longer periods of time. If it's abroad, somewhere you can embrace the language and culture. The places you enjoy visiting for two weeks may not be the place you want to live in for longer periods.

I have personally owned a property in Cyprus. Although I loved the property, on reflection, I missed the excitement of visiting new places. I always felt guilty travelling to another country as I was not then using the Cyprus property. I also resented the costs such as site management fees, rates and gardening costs as this was all a fixed expense regardless of the property being used and how long spent there. These costs soon add up, and perhaps could have funded a holiday elsewhere.

I am certainly not ruling out the idea of buying a property abroad again when I retire. however, I would prefer a different country. Whilst Cyprus is beautiful the flight times are longer than some of our European neighbours. Cyprus is also unlike other destinations with its all-year-round sunshine. I like the idea of France or Italy as I could enjoy the ski season in the winter and the sun in the summer. We can all dream!

I think it's important to highlight that a holiday home can be an expensive purchase. This can potentially use up a large portion of your overall wealth. If you use the holiday home as an exclusive asset for yourself, then it's a large amount of your capital that's not generating any income for you.

Some would debate that the income you are giving up will be saved against the money you would normally spend on holidays. This maybe the case, but remember, although a holiday home saves you accommodation costs, if the property is abroad you still have the costs of flights, and property maintenance.

I regularly meet clients who have the idea of buying a holiday home which they will use for themselves but also rent out for income. I think it's fair comment that a high percentage of these clients don't end up renting the property out. We can understandably become emotionally attached to a holiday home and therefore not want anyone else to use it.

For those who plan to purchase a holiday home and not rent it out, be sure you can afford to allocate so much capital in an asset that is not supporting your income needs in retirement.

Example alternative

I once met a client who was considering a holiday home in Portrush which would cost £300,000. He did not plan to rent it out so it would not generate any income. He planned to give up his annual holiday in Spain which cost him and his wife around £5000. However, he changed his mind.

He decided to purchase a caravan for £35,000. His view was that although the caravan would rapidly reduce in value, he could use the £265,000 remaining to purchase three smaller houses in his hometown to rent out.

The combined rental income on the three rented properties would generate around £2000 per month. Although the value of the caravan will eventually be worthless, he felt the value of the three properties would increase to offset this.

Although a holiday home of £300,000 should also grow similarly to the three rental properties, he felt he would get attached to the holiday home and not rent it out.

The potential rental income of £2,000 per month from three houses is £24,000 per year. Over a 10-year period this is £240,000. That's an enormous amount of income to give up over a 10-year period.

Although the caravan has site fees this was no greater than the fixed costs of the holiday home such as rates.

The view that the holiday home of £300,000 would save them £5,000 per year of holiday costs to Spain is fair. However, with this option they are losing out on £24,000 of rental income.

Whilst I appreciate a caravan is not for everyone, it does highlight that a holiday home not rented out is a luxury purchase. I think this should only be considered if you can be sure you're going to rent it out when you're not personally using it. If you're not going to rent it then you need to be sure you can you really afford to have this capital tied to a property giving up the potential income.

- Bucket list

When I ask retirees about a potential list of things they would like to do in their life, I find the answers are usually quite modest. I was unsure if this is a reflection of the modest Northern Ireland culture I live in or perhaps the UK in general.

A recent survey from Parkdean Resorts [28] compared the top 100 bucket list items from bucklist.net via Google search data from the last 12 months to determine which items have seen the most searches over the past year. This was particularly interesting given the pandemic we face at the time of writing. As you can see from the list, a lot of the activities don't cost significant amounts of money.

Ranking	Bucket List Idea
#1	Buy a car
#2	Donate blood
#3	Skydive
#4	Buy a house
#5	Scuba dive
#6	Write a book
#7	Learn to play guitar
#8	Learn French
#9	Learn sign language
#10	Fall in love

- Work around the house

For many of us we have countless things we never have got round to doing in our home. I would often argue you never finish decorating your home, it's an endless cycle of expense. Retirement is usually a point where many decide to tackle some home maintenance that's been put off for years.

Based on these suggestions take the time now and think about what expenses you may have in retirement.

3. How much inheritance do you want to leave?

Research conducted by the International Longevity Centre and Prudential in 2015 suggested that rather than spending our kids' inheritance, older people tend to spend less and save more.

Whilst the report confirms that in late retirement, we spend less due to our lifestyle changes, it also suggests the drive to hand over wealth to the next generation plays a part in this behavioural pattern. [29]

The report references the ELSA Wave Report from 2012/2013. This report showed on average 70% of people surveyed felt they had a chance of leaving a legacy in excess of £50,000.

Figure 24: Average expectation of leaving an inheritance of £50,000 or more

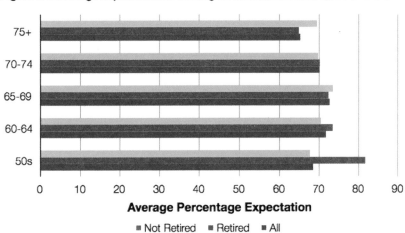

Source: ELSA Wave 6 (2012/13)

Our attitudes vary significantly in terms of leaving a legacy on death. Many retirees, particularly those with children, do have the desire to leave an inheritance upon their death. However, for some they take the view that having worked hard to accumulate savings, this money should all be theirs to spend. The latter view is certainly held more commonly by those without children.

Having taken time to understand your own expenditure needs, I recommend you also take the time to think about how much inheritance you would like to leave, if any.

From my experience of advising clients in this area over the past 20 years, I would make two simple observations.

- The more assets you want to leave behind, the less you have to spend potentially on yourself.

- I am yet to meet a client's family who wish their parents had left them more capital on death rather than spending capital with them during their lifetime creating memories.

I know without doubt that this second point is true for myself.

Why does this matter?

As mentioned, the aim of this book is to offer clarity, confidence and a sense of control.

For those who do wish to leave a legacy, by working out if it's affordable & realistic it removes the potential hesitation over enjoying your own savings with confidence. It allows you to spend your income as you have planned.

For those who hold a strong view about leaving a legacy, I think this question must go hand in hand with the question – how much I can spend in retirement. Simply put, leaving more behind means spending less when we are here.

Another question I am commonly asked would be, "I want to give my children money now: how much can I afford?"

Again, how can we comfortably give away gifts in our lifetime unless we feel completely in control of our own financial future? The question of giving money away in your lifetime or upon death can't really be answered without really understanding the impact it will have on your own lifestyle.

Interestingly, I regularly meet clients wanting to leave a legacy to their children, but by the same token rarely do those same clients want to count on a potential legacy from their own parents as part of their financial benefits in retirement.

We tend to have this drive to leave a legacy, but for the majority we hold this hesitance to even count upon what is likely to be inherited from our parents.

I would recommend reading The Intergenerational Commissions 2017 report titled 'The million dollar be-question' and the Royal London policy paper 'Will harassed "baby boomers' rescue Generation Rent?' (pp 30 & 31) Both of these reports offer a fascinating insight on our views around wealth and inheriting from and gifting to our family.

Don't forget that sometimes inheritance tax can erode the value of any gift on death. This is a specialist area of financial planning and you may require a professional to advise you.

List all your assets including properties, savings, investments and pension funds. How much on death do you feel should be left, if any?

4. How much guaranteed income will you have?

Even with the most carefully thought out retirement plan, it's inevitable that life will throw up a scenario we have not planned for.

Most financial advisors would agree that it's vital you always have enough guaranteed income to pay your normal household bills. When discussing your budget planner, we have encouraged you to separate your expenses into fixed, ad hoc and discretionary. An ideal retirement plan would ensure you have enough guaranteed income to cover at least all your fixed and ad hoc expenditure.

The main advantages of a guaranteed income include:

- Peace of mind to know the income will always be paid regardless of what's going on in the world.

- The income never runs out no matter how long you live. If you are living off capital, there is always the danger of overspending.

- Some of us are not as disciplined as others. A guaranteed income protects you from making a poor financial decision in later life.

- Although a guaranteed income could be deemed inflexible, it stops you changing your retirement plan later and making a wrong decision.

There are some disadvantages to guaranteed sources of income, and I shall cover these in the next chapter. Aside from the state pension the most common source of guaranteed income in retirement is a defined benefit pension, briefly discussed in an earlier chapter.

Before explaining this type of pension, let's take a step back and consider what a pension is. For the average person a pension is simply the income they live on in retirement. The pension is a consistent income that replaced their salary when they were working. Occasionally some retirees will describe a lump sum of savings built up over the years as their pension. We would refer to this lump sum as a pension pot.

Most pension pots today are built up through a pension within the workplace. These pension pots are a combination of payments from the employer, the employee and some tax incentives from the government.

Some pension pots are separate from the workplace, known as personal pensions. The three main reasons why this would happen are:

- You were self-employed.

- Your employer did not offer a pension.

- You preferred to have a pension pot that was different to that being offered through your employer.

These types of workplace pensions and personal pensions are known as defined contribution pensions.

Some retirees have accumulated additional lump sum savings or investments through alternative methods to a pension such as an ISA or even a basic savings account. These may still be seen as savings towards retirement and therefore still classed as their pension pot.

An ISA is an Individual Savings Account. The main benefit is that any interest earned is free from taxation. This is covered in more detail in chapter 4.

Whilst in all these examples the pension pot is not an income, this pool of money is intended to be turned into an income at the point of stopping work. Crucially, the level of income these pots produce and how long they last are your responsibility.

There are two pensions which will not build up a value in the same way as these pension pots but in fact will automatically pay a guaranteed income entitlement at retirement. These remove any responsibility from your shoulders by committing to pay the income for your lifetime.

The first is the basic state pension. The second are older and certainly fewer, known as defined benefit pensions.

I can remember working at Prudential as an 18-year-old and congratulating a 60-year-old colleague who was retiring. To celebrate his retirement and long service he was being presented with a gold watch. This type of gift was a tradition presented to employees who had served 25–30 years in the same company. I suppose the symbolic nature of this gift was that you have given such a large portion of your time to the company, in turn the company was recognising your time was now becoming your own.

The pension schemes of the past reflected this idea of rewarding long-standing employees for their years of service. These defined benefit pensions were designed so that the longer you served the company, the more income they would continue to pay when you retired.

With these pensions the employer carried the responsibility of providing you with a guaranteed income for life.

Example

Madison works for the same company for 30 years. When she retires her salary is £50,000.

An example defined benefit pension formula would be one sixtieth of final salary for every year worked.

Madison would have therefore built up 30 years or 30/60 of her final salary as a guaranteed income upon retirement. Her guaranteed income for life would be £25,000 per year.

Not all defined benefit pensions had the same formula, but they ultimately had the same concept of rewarding employees with a guaranteed income for life. The longer your service and higher your salary, the greater the guaranteed income at retirement.

As well as offering this guaranteed income, most schemes included a tax-free lump sum payment. Again, this payment normally increased in value with your length of service.

Many retirees today are benefiting from these guaranteed arrangements. So why do firms no longer offer these types of pensions?

There are two main reasons for this. Firstly, people are living much longer today. As retirees started living longer these guarantees were costing employers much more than expected. Life expectancy is covered in a lot more detail later in this chapter.

Secondly, investment returns have reduced. This matters as employers would set aside money each year to fund these guaranteed income payments. This money was set aside to grow in value which in turn helped the employer fund the income. Investment returns today are much lower than in the 70s and 80s. If there is less investment return, the employer needs to set aside more cash.

Some businesses have actually failed because the cost of income payments to retired employees had become unsustainable.

Although employers offering these schemes are now rare, public sector employees continue to enjoy the benefit.

The largest public sector schemes — such as the armed forces, civil service, NHS, firefighters, police and teachers — are all known as 'unfunded' schemes. This means that unlike the traditional method of employers building up a central pot to fund the payments, there's no central pot of money; instead, the government pays these incomes directly to retirees.

For most of the public, pension experts advise against transferring from these gold-plated final salary schemes due to their generous benefits.

The final throw of the dice

There is one other possibility which may yield results if you've not already tried it: tracking down lost insurance policies, pensions, shareholder register, which can be done easily via Experian's Unclaimed Assets Register: www.uar.co.uk There is a £25 charge to run a search but it trawls 4.5 million records from 80 different companies.

Alternatively, try the government's pension tracing service which will trace any missing pensions for you free of charge: www.gov.uk/find-lost-pension

For lost or government bank accounts, try: www.mylostaccount.org.uk

Your homework

Write down how much guaranteed income you will have when you retire. Include what date it would start. Also include any tax-free lump sum payments that are due.

How does this guaranteed income compare to your projected expenditure?

5. The impossible question: How long will you live?

When we reach retirement and begin to draw benefits from our pensions and investment, retirees generally fall into two distinct categories.

Firstly, those who are fortunate to hold enough guaranteed income or assets generating sufficient returns that meet their needs. Life expectancy is not as important for those in this position.

Example

Christine is aged 67 with pensions and investment pots worth £200,000. She has other pension income from her former employer of £1,000 per month along with a state pension of £700 per month. Christine feels she would need £1,940 per month to live a comfortable retirement. At present she is therefore £240 per month short of income.

Christine's £200,000 of pensions and investment funds are generating on average 3% per year. In monetary terms this equals £6,000 per year or £500 per month. These returns each year can comfortably pay £300 per month which after allowing for 20% income tax leaves £240 per month to cover Christine's income needs.

Should her assets continue to grow at this rate, Christine can continue to use this income for the rest of her life. Based on this 3% rate of return she will never erode the value of her £200,000; it will actually grow. Therefore, upon her death this capital can be passed down to her family.

Age	Investment	Withdrawal	Growth Rate	Year End
67	200,000	3,600	3.00%	202,292
68	202,292	3,600	3.00%	204,653
69	204,653	3,600	3.00%	207,084
70	207,084	3,600	3.00%	209,589
71	209,589	3,600	3.00%	212,169
72	212,169	3,600	3.00%	214,826
73	214,826	3,600	3.00%	217,562
74	217,562	3,600	3.00%	220,381
75	220,381	3,600	3.00%	223,285
76	223,285	3,600	3.00%	226,275
77	226,275	3,600	3.00%	229,355
78	229,355	3,600	3.00%	232,528
79	232,528	3,600	3.00%	235,796
80	235,796	3,600	3.00%	239,162
81	239,162	3,600	3.00%	242,629

Should nothing change in terms of Christine's income needs or the 3% return generated, Christine objectives will continually be met regardless of how long she lives.

If you're reading this example and feel you fall into this category, please be mindful that several other factors would need to be considered. These include but are not limited to the following:

- Inflation – Christine's expenses are £1,940 per month today, but the cost of living will rise.

- Variable growth rates – Although 3% maybe a realistic rate of return for Christine, based on her attitude to investment risk this would be an average. When investing it's likely these returns will be variable with some years lower and others higher.

- Market crash events – For Christine to achieve a 3% return it is likely her capital would be invested. Based on historical events it would be prudent to stress test any future plans to allow for further years of volatile investment markets, such as the current Covid-19 pandemic which we are living through at the time of writing.

- Pensions increases – It is possible that Christine's company pension and state pension will increase each year to help keep pace with the increase in expenses.

- Life changes – Christine may have changing circumstances that mean her financial goals change.

- Taxation – tax rates can increase or decrease leaving us feeling better or worse off.

All these points will be explained in more detail later under the section Cashflow Forecasting.

For retirees not in this position, this next example illustrates when life expectancy becomes of much greater importance. Should we need to withdraw more from our pensions and investments than they make each year, the position changes. This scenario results in the need for us to use our capital each year to help support our income.

Example

If we continue with Christine from the previous example. Rather than Christine needing £300 per month, she has decided she needs £1,250 per month before tax (£15,000 per year) from her £200,000 of pensions & investment pot. Assuming her assets continue to earn 3% per year let's look at the impact this has on Christine.

This simple cashflow forecast shows that Christine is now spending some of her own capital along with the returns each year.

Age	Investment	Withdrawal	Growth Rate	Year End
67	200,000	15,000	3.00%	190,550
68	190,550	15,000	3.00%	180,817
69	180,817	15,000	3.00%	170,791
70	170,791	15,000	3.00%	160,465
71	160,465	15,000	3.00%	149,829
72	149,829	15,000	3.00%	138,874
73	138,874	15,000	3.00%	127,590
74	127,590	15,000	3.00%	115,967
75	115,967	15,000	3.00%	103,996
76	103,996	15,000	3.00%	91,666
77	91,666	15,000	3.00%	78,966
78	78,966	15,000	3.00%	65,885
79	65,885	15,000	3.00%	52,412
80	52,412	15,000	3.00%	38,534
81	38,534	15,000	3.00%	24,240
82	24,240	15,000	3.00%	9,517
83	9,517	9,517	3.00%	0

In this example Christine has now run out of money at age 82. Should she live beyond that age, her life will be financially more difficult.

The most recent past and projected period life tables released by the Office of National Statics had the following findings: [32]

- Baby boys born in the UK in 2018 can expect to live on average to 87.6 years old and girls to 90.2 years old, considering projected changes in mortality patterns over their lifetime.

- In 25 years, cohort life expectancy at birth in the UK is projected to increase by 2.8 years to reach 90.4 years for boys and by 2.4 years to 92.6 years for girls born in 2043.

- People aged 65 years in the UK in 2018 can expect to live on average a further 19.9 years for males and 22.0 years for females, projected to rise to 22.2 years for males and 24.2 years for females in 2043.

- In 2043 in the UK, 20.8% of new-born boys and 26.1% of new-born girls are expected to live to at least 100 years of age, an increase from 13.6% for boys and 18.2% for girls born in 2018.

- In comparison with the 2016-based projections, cohort life expectancy at birth is 2.6 years lower for males and 2.7 years lower for females in 2043 than previously projected.

The Office of National Statistics (ONS) website has a life expectancy calculator which you can use to project your own average lifespan.

Some financial services providers have attempted to take this calculation a step further. Both Aviva and Just Retirement offer a similar calculator by adjusting your estimated life expectancy according to your health.

It's worth mentioning too that the ONS also produces data on how life expectancy changes depending on your post code. Perhaps this is food for thought when you consider your next house move!

Who else is interested in how long we might live?

As mentioned earlier, pension schemes can be divided into two main types: a defined benefit pension or a defined contribution pension.

A Defined Benefit (DB) pension plan sets out the specific pension benefit that will be paid to a retiree. This calculation considers factors such as the number of years an employee has worked and their salary, which then dictate the pension and/or lump sum that will be paid on retirement.

Defined Benefit pension plans are sometimes known as Final Salary pension schemes or career average pensions. They're always workplace pensions arranged by your employer.

A Defined Benefit pension crucially not only offers you a guaranteed income for life after retirement, but usually indexed (increasing) to keep up with the cost of living.

Remember, under a Defined Benefit Pension, the scheme carries the responsibility and worry of paying this agreed guaranteed income for life.

The longer we live the more the pension scheme must pay out. For this reason, employers offering Defined Benefit pensions need to understand how long the average male and female is likely to live. This is known as longevity risk.

A Defined Contribution pension can be either workplace pensions arranged by your employer or private pensions, which you arrange yourself and pay into separately from any employer. This might be the option you choose if you're self-employed, for instance.

Under a Defined Contribution pension the amount of income payable at retirement is your own responsibility. Quite simply you are responsible for ensuring that the value of this pension pot is enough to support your income needs for the remainder of your life.

At this point, if you revisit the earlier example of Christine. In the first scenario her fund would last for life regardless of how long she lives. In the second example she would run out of money at 82. Clearly the length of Christine's life is very important in terms of deciding how much money she can afford to spend each year.

For those retirees with Defined Contribution pension pots, upon retirement there are two main methods of using these funds to support your retirement. These will be covered in a lot more detail in the next chapter, but it's important to highlight them now to reinforce the importance of considering how long we may live.

The different methods of using a Defined Contribution pension each have advantages and disadvantages. Everyone has their own circumstances to be considered when deciding which solution is best. In some situations, a combination of methods may be the most suitable solution.

The first method could be summarised as a flexible income where you take from your pension as and when required. Ultimately, with a flexible pension income the retiree carries the responsibility for ensuring the capital provides what they need throughout their lifetime.

In the example of Christine earlier she is using a form of flexible pension income.

The second method which retirees can use is an annuity.

An annuity is a retirement income product that you buy with some or all of your pension pot. It pays a regular retirement income either for life or for a set period. As with a defined benefit pension, it offers the peace of mind to know the level of income is certain. The responsibility rests with an insurance company to ensure the income is paid.

Annuities are retirement income products sold by insurance companies. They are contracts between the individual and the insurance company. The contract binds the insurance company to pay a certain level of income in exchange for a fixed sum of capital.

How much retirement income you will get from an annuity is ultimately driven by how long the insurance company feel you are likely to live.

Insurance company actuaries rely on lots of information to help project our likely lifespan. They of course need to be careful with these projections as they are committed to paying this income for the rest of your life, and how profitable this arrangement is for the annuity provider depends on how long you live.

When purchasing an annuity how long you may live is of upmost interest to the annuity provider. With the commitment to often pay an income for life if everyone suddenly started living 20 years longer than historical averages these arrangements may not be very profitable for the Insurance company.

Your family history is an important consideration for insurance companies when thinking about your longevity. Genetics will play a part in our likely longevity.

Your own health history is another clue as we now have lots of information showing how various conditions can reduce our own life expectancy.

Once you buy an annuity you can't change your mind, so it's important to get help and advice before committing to one.

It's also worth mentioning that those who have not chosen an annuity but instead to have a flexible pension income it is possible to purchase an annuity later using the value of the pot remaining at the time of annuity purchase.

Example

Lynn's Defined Contribution pension is worth £200,000. She is age 60 and just about to retire. Lynn has a company pension from a previous employer which is £700 per month (£8,400 per year) and she would like an extra income of £600 per month to live on. Lynn does not feel she could pay all her bills on less than a total of £1300 per month.

Lynn uses the £200,000 pension to purchase an annuity. The Insurance company agrees to pay £656 per month (£7,872 per year which is a 3.9% return) for the rest of Lynn's life. When she passes away the payments on this annuity cease.

Remember Lynn is allowed to earn £12,500 per year without paying income tax. This payment of £7,872, when added to her £8,400 company pension, would give a total income of £16,272.

Therefore, £3,772 of her income is above the £12,500 personal allowance and taxable at 20% tax. Lynn will lose £754.40 per year in income tax.

This leaves her with a total income after tax of £15,517.60 or £1,293.13 per month.

If Lynn had purchased the annuity but five years later, at age 65, the £200,000 would pay an income of £9,165 per year (4.58% return). This is an extra £1,293 more that the quote at age 60. This extra income is because Lynn is five years older and therefore the insurance company will not be paying her for as long.

It's a question that no one can answer: how long are you likely to live?

Visit the Office of National Statistics website. If you have had some health conditions in the past why not find out if any statistics suggest this could change your average life expectancy.

6. What other assets and potential income will you have at retirement?

As explained, your state pension, along with any Defined Benefit pension income, can form a significant part of your income needs at retirement. However, you may have other potential sources of income as well. Although these may not be a guaranteed, they may consistently pay an income which supports your needs in retirement. Examples include:

- Continued part-time employment
- Income from a business or self-employment
- State benefits in addition to your basic state pension
- Regular income received from a parent or indeed a family trust
- Rental income from land or property

Looking at these suggestions, list the guaranteed income included from question 4 and any other regular sources of income you may receive in retirement. Specifically, include how much you anticipate this to be and how often it will be received. If applicable, note the date the income is likely to end.

Income Source	Amount	Frequency	End Date

In addition to this extra income, you may have other pots, whether in defined contribution pensions or other savings and investments. These pots may also be used to help fund your income & capital needs at retirement.

You might also expect to inherit a future windfall such as an inheritance. Should you wish to include this as part of your overall retirement plan, this can also be included here.

List all of your cash-based savings accounts including any Cash ISAs & National Savings such as Premium Bonds.

Provider	Type of Account	Interest Rate	Maturity Date	Penalties

For each of your investments it's important to establish the following information:

1. The rate of return
- How much has it grown in value over the past year?
- What is the overall return since the investment was originally made?
- Does this rate of return change or is it fixed?

2. Penalties
- Are there any penalties for withdrawing money?
- If so, is there a date after which these penalties won't apply?

3. Restrictions
- Are there any restrictions on how often or the amount you can withdraw?
- Can you turn on a regular income?

4. Tax
- Are there any tax implications involved with withdrawing money?*

   *This can be a particularly complicated area and you may need to seek advice.

5. Charges
- Do any management charges apply?
- If yes, how much are these costs?

It can be difficult sometimes to obtain all of this information. For some it can be complicated, and at times feel overwhelming. This information is essential, however, in understanding how best these funds should be used as part of your retirement plan.

If you don't feel comfortable obtaining this information, consider seeking advice from a suitable qualified financial advisor.

Provider					
Type of Investment					
Return over last 12 months					
Overall Return					
Penalties					
Restrictions					
Tax					
Charges					

When considering any defined contribution pensions, it's important to establish the same questions described for investments. However, trying to establish the tax position when withdrawing from your pension is very dependent on which of the various options you use.

I have included a similar table at this point to capture any of your existing defined contribution pensions excluding taxation and methods of withdrawal. These will be covered in more detail in the next chapter.

It's also important to establish if these contracts hold any hidden features. This is because some older pensions in particular hold valuable benefits that are often overlooked.

Guaranteed annuity rate

As mentioned earlier an annuity is an agreement between you and an insurance company. This contract commits the insurance company to provide you with an income in exchange for a lump sum normally built up in your pension pot.

The amount of income you are likely to be offered at the time of retirement from an annuity is dependent on a number of factors - a principal one being interest rates. A lower interest rate leads to a lower annuity rate. The lower the interest rate is at the time you purchase your annuity, the less income you're likely to secure.

Some pensions have a pre-agreed annuity rate built into the contract. This means at retirement, sometimes a specific age, the annuity rate offered will be a pre-agreed rate rather than the rate available in the wider market. Given the significant fall in interest rates over recent years, these guaranteed annuity rates can be attractive to a retiree. I have no doubt several insurance companies now regret offering these arrangements as they are proving to be very expensive.

If you have a guaranteed annuity rate, a simple way to check if it's a valuable benefit is to compare the rate on offer in the open market with other annuity providers. They will need your age and medical history. There are different types of annuity, about which I shall explain more in the next chapter. It's important to note that although guaranteed annuity rates can seem attractive, they can be inflexible in that the type of annuity can't be changed.

Guaranteed growth rates

Some pensions offer a guaranteed rate of increase each year. I have frequently seen pension contracts with a guaranteed 4% annual return. In a climate with interest rates so low, any contract with this level of guaranteed return should only be given up with careful consideration.

It can be a complicated process trying to understand if your pension holds these benefits and exactly what are the guarantees on offer. In my experience some pension providers can be extremely slow in establishing if the contract holds any guarantees.

If you are feeling unsure, it is best to seek the advice of a pension specialist who understands exactly how these guarantees work. In addition, how are these going to be of value to you based on your own circumstances?

Provider					
Type of pension					
Return over the last 12 month					
Overall return					
Penalties					
Charges					

A final and important question to consider at this point: What impact would drawing from any of these pension or investment pots have on any state benefits of which you are in receipt?

7. Compromise – What could you give up in retirement if you had to?

In an ideal world you will be able to live out your perfect retirement.

Unfortunately for some, they won't have the income and capital to do this. I must admit, certainly over the past 10 years, I can't remember meeting a client for whom this was the case. I find most people are modest in their financial expectations. Perhaps they already have a sense of what is realistic before having this discussion. However, if you had to give up anything listed in questions 1, 2 and 3, what would it be?

Chapter 6

Options at retirement – part 2

"These Freedoms are based on the simple idea that people know better how to spend their own money than governments do." George Osborne, Chancellor of the Exchequer.

Taking benefits from your pension – introduction

In 2015, the Chancellor George Osborne made radical changes to the pension landscape.

These reforms would allow pension savers to access their defined contribution pension pots once they reached age 55. From this point on they could take as much money from their pension as they liked; the previous restrictions which forced retirees to use their pension solely to provide an income through an annuity were removed. As Mr Osborne said at the time, "No one will have to buy an annuity." [33]

These changes to pensions took everyone by surprise. Not everyone agreed with them. Many argued that the previous regime encouraged savers to build up an income for life with the government offering generous tax benefits as an incentive – the idea being that if a greater percentage of the public provided their own guaranteed income for life, fewer would need financial support from the state.

Pension Minister at the time Steve Webb was famously asked the question: Did he not worry that some would take all their pension money and buy a Lamborghini? He answered that if someone wanted to spend all their pension on a Lamborghini and live on state pension, that was their choice. [34]

Annuities had certainly lost popularity by 2015. Falling interest rates had meant that they had become much more expensive. This graph shows how much less income a £100,000 annuity purchased today would pay compared with previous years. [35] Perhaps this is one of the reasons George Osborne introduced these new freedoms.

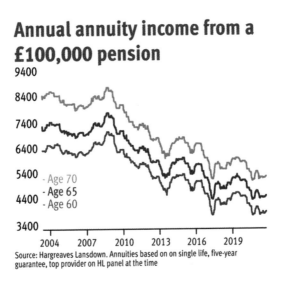

Annual annuity income from a £100,000 pension

- Age 70
- Age 65
- Age 60

2004 2007 2010 2013 2016 2019

Source: Hargreaves Lansdown. Annuities based on on single life, five-year guarantee, top provider on HL panel at the time

Giving people at retirement the choice on how to spend their own money has advantages. With these advantages comes responsibility.

Looking back since these changes, early indicators suggest we are enjoying this newfound freedom. Whilst not buying Lamborghinis, a recent report by People Pension suggests we could be spending more than we can afford. The report shows that 74% of those interviewed are in danger of running out of money in their early to mid-eighties. [36] A report by the World Economic Forum also recently highlighted similar findings. Most of these people are not getting any regular financial advice.

It could be that those surveyed are enjoying their earlier retirement years while they have the health and energy to do so. However, if they have spent all their pension pots by their mid-eighties, will their remaining guaranteed sources of income be enough to live on?

One unintended consequence of these new rules has also been an increase in pension scams. Over £30 million has been lost since 2017 in pension scams. Amounts being scammed have ranged from £1000 to £500,000 with the average victim being males in their fifties. Action Fraud's latest campaign on this topic urges the public to be careful and seek impartial advice. [37]

Defined benefit pensions options

Defined benefit pensions are subject to their own individual scheme rules. As such, the changes to pensions in 2015 have not altered these types of pensions. Upon retirement, within a defined benefit pension the income is already pre-defined. The pension amount will be directly linked to your earnings and number of years' service. This income will be paid for the rest of your life.

As we age, we can all look back on certain items that used to be cheaper than they are today. This is known as inflation.

To help ensure retirees don't feel worse off as costs increase, many pensions will also increase in value so as the amount of income from their defined benefit pension keeps pace with the cost of living. This again will already be pre-agreed within the terms of the pension scheme. Ask for a copy of your pension scheme booklet if you're unsure how your own scheme will work in this respect.

I must stress this is a very valuable benefit, as illustrated below. If your pension did not increase in value with inflation, you would feel the effect. Have a look at the websites 'NerdWallet' and 'Candid Money'(38 & 39). They have excellent calculators which help demonstrate just how much inflation has increased the cost of goods and services we buy.

Example

From the Candid Money Historic Calculator.

If I purchased a pair of shoes for £50 in the year 2000, and these increased in price in line with the average rate of inflation of 2.7%, the same shoes would cost £76.76 in 2016.

Another aspect of a defined benefit scheme over which a retiree has no control is what happens to your pension income upon death. Most defined pension schemes will continue to pay a percentage of your pension income upon death to your spouse or civil partner. Some will also guarantee the income is paid at the same level as you receive for a fixed period after your death, known as a guarantee period.

Should you pass away and have a young family, some schemes will pay a dependant's pension to your children. Again, information on death benefits will be in the scheme booklet.

Example

Jenny has just passed away after retiring three years ago. Her pension was £1,500 per month. Upon death, her pension will continue to be paid at £1,500 per month to her husband for another two years. After this her husband will receive £750 per month for the rest of his life. This £750 monthly payment will increase each year by 2% to help keep up with inflation.

With so much pre-defined already within a defined benefit pension, upon retirement retirees don't have many options to choose from. However, one decision they will face is how much tax-free cash to take, if any.

When you start drawing benefits from a defined benefit pension you may be able to draw some benefits as a tax-free lump sum. This can also be known as a pension commencement lump sum. The scheme rules will determine how much you can receive as a lump sum.

Should you decide to take some of your entitlement as a tax-free lump sum you will in turn need to reduce some of the pension income you are entitled to. The amount of pension income exchanged for a tax-free lump sum is decided by a 'commutation factor' which the pension scheme offers. This is the level of tax-free lump sum you will get for every £1000 of annual pension income you forgo.

Example

Arnold is approaching retirement and due to receive £10,000 per year of pension from his defined benefit pension scheme. Arnold has been informed his scheme has a commutation factor of 15. If the scheme rules permitted, Arnold could take £8,000 per year as a pension, then he could receive £30,000 of a tax-free lump sum.

This is calculated as the commutation factor is 15. This means he will receive £15 tax free lump sum for every £1 of annual pension he gives up.

Therefore, in this example he is giving up £2,000 x 15 = £30,000.

It's important to note that you can't normally exchange all your pension for a tax-free lump sum. The amount will usually be capped by the rules of the scheme. This information is available within the pension scheme booklet.

HMRC also set out an overall cap on the maximum entitlement to a tax-free lump sum payment for any individual. It would be unlikely that any pension scheme rules would permit more commutation of income in exchange for a lump sum than the tax-free amount permitted by HMRC.

There are pros and cons of taking the maximum tax-free lump sum.

Some of the advantages are as follows:

- The obvious benefit is that the payment is tax free. If you draw a regular pension income, it's taxable. Therefore, any income above the personal allowance of £12,500 is subject to income tax at 20%.

A reminder that the personal allowance is the amount of income you can earn before paying any income tax.

Example

Stuart has just received his pension entitlement from his employer as he is about to retire. He can take a regular pension of £13,570. As this is his only source of income, he will pay tax on £1,070 of this (£13,570 – £12,500 personal allowance).

Stuart would pay 20% income tax on the £1,070 above the personal allowance, meaning he will lose £214 per year of tax.

Stuart's pension allows him to commute £1,000 of his income in exchange for £15,000 of lump sum. Although Stuart's giving up £1,000 of income, he is only really giving up £786 of this as the other £214 would have been lost in tax.

- The ability to use the lump sum to cater for any additional costs.

- As we've discussed, some will want to leave a legacy to their family upon death. A defined benefit pension normally pays a continuing income to your spouse, civil partner or dependants. This income will stop at some pre-defined point in future, such as the death of your spouse.

- Some they may prefer to leave a lump sum on death rather than a regular income. Others may want to leave a legacy beyond their immediate family such as their grandchildren. The defined benefit pension may not include this person(s) as permitted to inherit a continuing income within its scheme rules. As such, exchanging a pension income for a lump sum could go some way to achieving the objective of leaving a lump sum legacy on death.

Example

Kelvin wants to know whether when he dies his grandson Jack will get an inheritance. Kelvin's pension entitlement is £10,000 per year. He has no spouse as his wife died 10 years earlier. His children are all in their 40s and the pension he has does not consider anyone to be a dependant unless they are your own children and under the age of 23.

Upon death, Kelvin's £10,000 per year pension would stop and no further income payments made because he has no spouse or dependants: grandchildren are not classed as dependants.

Kelvin can take a reduced pension of £8,000 per year and a tax-free lump sum of £30,000. If Kelvin feels the £8,000 per year pension is enough, he could use all or part of the £30,000 tax-free lump sum as a future inheritance for Jack.

- Even for those who can't afford to give up pension income, the tax-free lump sum can be invested to generate further income. This can be useful particularly for those who sadly have poor health or a reduced life expectancy due to illness.

Example

Continuing the example of Kelvin: Prior to taking his pension, Kelvin is sadly diagnosed with a terminal illness. The doctors estimate he has five years to live. Should Kelvin take the full pension of £10,000 per year, over five years he will have extracted £50,000 of benefit.

However, let's imagine Kelvin takes the reduced income of £8,000 and a tax-free lump sum of £30,000. During these five years Kelvin invests the £30,000 into an ISA. This earns a 4% return on the ISA every year, totalling £1,200 per year. He can use this £1,200 per year to add to his £8,000 pension, making his combined income £9,200 per year. This is only £800 less than the full pension of £10,000.

Although the 4% income for the ISA is not guaranteed, should this be achieved Kelvin is only giving up £800 of income. Over the five years, he will have earned £76,000 (£8,000 x 5 years + £30,000 lump sum + £6,000 return on the ISA).

This is £26,000 more than simply taking the £10,000 per year pension.

Although beyond the scope of this book, pension experts would agree Kelvin should consider a full transfer of his defined benefit pension due to his short life span. Given his short life expectancy, this could further improve the benefits on death. Financial planning is mandatory in this situation as a defined benefit pension can't be transferred without financial advice if the transfer value is over £30,000.

Although for some it makes sense to commute some of their benefits, there are some disadvantages:

- As highlighted, pensions will normally increase in payment each year. When you give up some of your pension for a lump sum, you are in effect giving up the future increases that this pension income would also have gained.

Example

Arnold has given up £2,000 per year of pension in exchange for £30,000 of a lump sum. Arnold's pension in payment would rise each year by 2%. If Arnold is aged 60 when he retires, consider how much the £2,000 would have been worth at age 75 when we include the 2% annual increase. The income would have totalled £2,692 per year.

- By taking tax-free cash you are reducing the level of monthly income. In some cases, based on your income needs this may not be affordable. I have met some clients in the past who don't need any more capital as they have set aside cash already for these purposes. However, the same clients also needed every penny of guaranteed income to meet their expenditure needs.

Example

Tony needs £20,000 per year to live in retirement. He feels that even living on this level of income could be difficult. Tony has the choice of a £20,000-per-year pension or a £16,000 annual pension and a £60,000 tax-free lump sum. Tony does not see the need for any extra capital in future as the £60,000 in saving will be more than enough. Tony has no health issues to suggest he won't live a long healthy life. Tony is single and does not have anyone to whom he wishes to leave a legacy.

Although the £60,000 could be invested and generate some return, Tony needs £20,000 as a minimum to live on just to pay his bills.

Tony decides that although the £60,000 could be used to generate a return and could be used to top up the £4,000 shortfall, he does not want the risk that this does not happen. He prefers the security of the £20,000 income guaranteed for the rest of his life.

- Although it may look affordable to have a lower income today in exchange for a lump sum. It is also important to consider what death benefits your partner will need upon your death. If you reduce your income today, this will reduce the income payable to your spouse or civil partner on death.

Example

Michael is married to Louise. Michael is about to retire and has built up a generous pension of £40,000 per year from his employer, having spent 30 years working with the same firm. Louise has stayed at home raising their four children and therefore has no company pension entitlement other than the basic state pension of £179.60 per week.

Michael can take a reduced pension of £32,000 per year and £120,000 tax-free lump sum. Michael likes the idea of this option to gift each of his children a lump sum of £30,000 as a deposit for their first homes.

Michael's pension will pay a 50% spouse pension to Louise upon his death. We have calculated that Louise needs £28,000 of total income to live a comfortable lifestyle should Michael die.

If Michael takes the maximum £40,000 pension option, upon his death Louise will receive £20,000 for the rest of her life (50% of £40,000). When added to her state pension (£179.60 per week x 52 weeks = £9,339.20), her total income will be £29,339.20 which would be more than enough to meet her target income of £28,000.

However, should Michael choose the option of the maximum tax-free lump sum, Louise would receive £16,000 of Michael's pension (50% of £32,000 = £16,000). When added to her state pension this leaves a total income of £25,339.20. This would cause a problem for Louise as it's less than the £28,000 we have calculated that she needs.

- The commutation factor on offer can vary between schemes. A higher commutation factor represents better value for money. The lower the factor the less valuable the benefit.

For those mathematicians who perhaps still can't decide and want to choose the option that offers 'best value', ultimately each commutation factor represents good or bad value depending on how long you live. I have run a calculator to illustrate. This is based on Arnold, our 60-year-old male, who has been offered a pension of £10,000 per year going up by 2% each year. He can commute £2,000 of his pension in exchange for £30,000 tax-free lump sum.

This calculation assumes Arnold does not need the £30,000 for any purpose but invests the money and earns a 2% return each year. The calculation also assumes Arnold pays 20% tax on his income. He uses the lump sum of £30,000 to top up the £2,000 income he has lost. He therefore now has £8,000 income from this pension and uses £2,000 from the lump sum each year.

Age	Full Pension	Cumulative Full Pension	Reduced Pension	Cumulative Red Pen	Cumulative Difference		PCLS	Annual Difference	Fund year End
60	8,000.00	8,000.00	6,400.00	6,400.00	1,600.00		30,000.00	1,600.00	29,110.00
61	8,160.00	16,160.00	6,528.00	12,928.00	3,232.00		29,110.00	1,632.00	28,164.95
62	8,323.20	24,483.20	6,658.56	19,586.56	4,896.64		28,164.95	1,664.64	27,162.82
63	8,489.66	32,972.86	6,791.73	26,378.29	6,594.57		27,162.82	1,697.93	26,101.51
64	8,659.46	41,632.32	6,927.57	33,305.86	8,326.46		26,101.51	1,731.89	24,978.86
65	8,832.65	50,464.97	7,066.12	40,371.97	10,092.99		24,978.86	1,766.53	23,792.63
66	9,009.30	59,474.27	7,207.44	47,579.41	11,894.85		23,792.63	1,801.86	22,540.54
67	9,189.49	68,663.75	7,351.59	54,931.00	13,732.75		22,540.54	1,837.90	21,220.21
68	9,373.28	78,037.03	7,498.62	62,429.62	15,607.41		21,220.21	1,874.66	19,829.20
69	9,560.74	87,597.77	7,648.59	70,078.21	17,519.55		19,829.20	1,912.15	18,364.98
70	9,751.96	97,349.72	7,801.56	77,879.78	19,469.94		18,364.98	1,950.39	16,824.95
71	9,946.99	107,296.72	7,957.60	85,837.37	21,459.34		16,824.95	1,989.40	15,206.44
72	10,145.93	117,442.65	8,116.75	93,954.12	23,488.53		15,206.44	2,029.19	13,506.68
73	10,348.85	127,791.51	8,279.08	102,233.20	25,558.30		13,506.68	2,069.77	11,722.84
74	10,555.83	138,347.34	8,444.66	110,677.87	27,669.47		11,722.84	2,111.17	9,851.96
75	10,766.95	149,114.28	8,613.56	119,291.43	29,822.86		9,851.96	2,153.39	7,891.04
76	10,982.29	160,096.57	8,785.83	128,077.25	32,019.31		7,891.04	2,196.46	5,836.94
77	11,201.93	171,298.50	8,961.55	137,038.80	34,259.70		5,836.94	2,240.39	3,686.47
78	11,425.97	182,724.47	9,140.78	146,179.58	36,544.89		3,686.47	2,285.19	1,436.31
79	11,654.49	194,378.96	9,323.59	155,503.17	38,875.79		1,436.31	1,436.31	0.00
80	11,887.58	206,266.54	9,510.06	165,013.23	41,253.31		0.00	0.00	0.00

In this example, if Arnold lives to age 80, his tax-free cash will have run out and his only source of income will be his reduced pension. Should Arnold live longer than age 80, he would have been better off taking the maximum income and no tax-free lump sum.

This example is starting to get more complicated, and indeed subject to many variables such as the return on the investment and the rate of income tax. Should you feel you need an analysis of whether your tax-free lump sum commutation represents good value of money, it is best to seek the expertise of a professional financial planner.

Trivial commutation

A final note on the options for defined benefit pensions. Should the total value of all your pension benefits fall below £30,000, the entire value of the pension can be exchanged for a lump sum. This means no income will be paid as a pension and all the benefit is payable in the form of a one-off lump sum.

Example

Ruben has no pension arrangements other than a small benefit built up through a few years with a former employer. The total value of this pension benefit is a projected pension of £1,000 per year. Ruben has been given the option to take the entire pot which is worth £20,000.

If Ruben chooses this option, 25% of the pot will be tax free (£20,000 x 25% = £5000). The remaining £15,000 will be added to Ruben's other taxable income in that financial year. Ruben still works and earns £20,000 per year. This £15,000 will be taxed at 20% as his total income is £35,000. Therefore, in this example Ruben will lose £3,000 in tax (£15,000 x 20%) leaving him with a lump sum of £17,000 and no further pension payments.

How secure is your defined benefit pension?

This is a question we are often asked. Some retirees worry about the possibility of losing this guaranteed income due to financial difficulties encountered by their former employer.

The Pension Protection Fund (PPF) protects people with a defined benefit pension when an employer becomes insolvent. If the employer doesn't have enough funds to pay you the pension they promised, the PPF will provide compensation instead.

If your pension scheme qualifies, the amount of compensation you get depends on whether you had passed your normal pension age when your employer became insolvent.

Anyone receiving survivor's pensions, such as widows, widowers, children, civil partners etc will also normally qualify for 100% of the pension income.

If you were over your normal pension age or started drawing your pension early due to ill-health, you're entitled to receive a full pension from the PPF.

If you were under your normal pension age, you're entitled to receive a pension of 90% of the amount you've built up when your employer became insolvent. This is also subject to an upper cap set by the government.

For example, the cap from 1 April 2021 up to and including 31 March 2022 for a 65-year-old is £41,461.07 per annum.

The PPF was set up by the government in April 2005 and protects millions of people throughout the UK.

If you were a member of a defined benefit pension before April 2005, you might be protected by the Financial Assistance Scheme (FAS).

FAS was set up to protect members who had defined benefits where:

- the employer became insolvent before 28 February 2006.

- the pension scheme came to an end between 1 January 1997 and 5 April 2005.

- the pension scheme couldn't afford to pay those benefits promised to members.

FAS benefits are regarded as compensation and are paid in the form of a top-up. This aims to provide members with 90% of the defined benefit pension that they would have received at their normal pension age. This is up to a cap of £36,901 a year in the 2021/22 tax year.

If you're unable to work because of ill health, the FAS can make payments before your normal retirement age, but there might be some restrictions.

Options for defined contribution pension pots

For those retirees who have accumulated pension pots at retirement, they are faced with the choice and responsibility of how best these should be used. This is the area that has been impacted the most by the pension freedom rules introduced by George Osborne in 2015.

The starting point for deciding how to use these pots is by considering your monthly expenditure needs. Secondly, we need to take this likely monthly expenditure and compare this figure to what guaranteed monthly income you will have.

Identifying if there is a shortfall between guaranteed income and total expenditure is vital before deciding how best to use your defined contribution pots. This is known as the 'safety first' option.

Example

Jessie is aged 65. She has gone through her likely monthly expense in retirement and identified she will need £2,000 per month. Her state pension

& defined benefit pensions combined will generate £1,700 per month. She has £100,000 in defined contribution pension pots.

Jessie needs to ensure the £100,000 pot tops up her income by £300 per month for the rest of her life.

Jessie has had good health and her parents and grandparents all lived beyond 80 years old.

Tax-free cash option

In a similar way to the defined benefit pension, defined contribution pension pots allow retirees to take a tax-free lump sum. This is usually more straightforward to calculate, as in most cases this is a standard 25% of the pot value.

Therefore, in the above example Jessie could take £25,000 of her pot as a tax-free lump sum.

The advantages & disadvantages of taking your tax-free cash from a defined contribution pension don't differ from those described previously under defined benefit schemes.

Annuity purchase

For those like Jessie who don't have enough guaranteed income to meet their needs, they can consider an annuity. By using all or part of their defined contribution pot they can secure a regular guaranteed income for life.

This is an exchange between the retiree, who is giving up a lump sum within his pension pot, and an insurance company, that will pay the retiree a guaranteed income for life. This is like buying your own defined benefit pension income.

In 2015 when pension regulations changed, George Osborne said at the time, "No one will have to buy an annuity." That does not mean annuities represent a poor financial choice for everyone. For some the purchase of one will form part of their pension income strategy at retirement. What these new rules mean is that those who <u>don't need</u> an annuity won't be forced to purchase one.

If we take the example of Jessie, she may want to use a portion of her £100,000 pension pot to get the extra £300 per month of guaranteed income that she needs.

If Jessie was aged 65 and used £75,000 to purchase a single life annuity, the annual income would be £3,652 (based on rates at the time of writing). Divided over a 12-month period this would generate just over the £300 per month. This is an annuity rate of 4.87% (£75,000 x 4.87% = £3652)

The annuity rate depends on several factors, one of which would include interest rates. Annuity rates tend to follow interest rates indirectly. The current Bank of England interest rate is 0.1% – the lowest on record. In 2008 the Bank of England interest rate was 5%. If you consider the diagram earlier in this chapter, you can see the decline in annuity rates follows the pattern of declining UK interest rates.

Obviously, age impacts on the annuity rate. If we change Jessie's age to 70, the same £75,000 single life annuity would pay £4,210 per year, an increase of £558 per year. This represents an annuity rate of 5.61%. The higher annuity rate reflecting that Jessie is older and thus the insurer will pay this for 5 years less than the example at age 65.

In this example I have kept the choice of annuity simple. However, when choosing an annuity, we have quite a number of options that can be useful to the retiree and will influence the annuity rate offered by the insurer.

The main options when selecting an annuity that significantly impact on the amount of annuity you will are as follows:

Frequency

You can normally have your annuity income paid monthly, quarterly, half yearly or yearly.

Advance or arrears

You can opt to have your income paid in advance or arrears. This simply means at the start or end of your chosen frequency. If you choose monthly in advance, your first payment would be made immediately after purchasing the annuity. Monthly in arrears would mean your first payment is paid one month after purchasing the annuity.

Joint life

Rather than purchase an annuity on your own life, which would end upon your death. A joint life annuity can be useful for those in a relationship. This allows all or part of your annuity income to be paid to your spouse or partner in the event of your death. You can decide at what level your income would continue to be paid. This can be 100%, 67% or 50% of your pension income. The higher the figure you want paid after your death, the lower the annuity you will be offered by the insurer.

If you consider Jessie again, on the original annuity example she was offered £3,652 per year. We have now added a male partner of the same age and requested that **100%** of the income continues to be paid to him after Jessie's death.

This results in the lifetime income being reduced to £3,132 per year. This represents a reduction of £520 from an annuity on Jessie's life only (£3652 − £3132 = £520 per year). This is due to the insurance company potentially having to pay the income for longer as it won't stop until <u>both</u> have died.

The decision to include a joint life on an annuity purchase should be driven by your needs rather than the perceived value – that is to say, your and your partner's understanding of what their expenditure is likely to mean for their income needs after your death. If a shortfall exists, a joint life annuity should be strongly considered.

If for example on Jessie's death the income does not need to continue at the same level, instead she asks for only 50% of the income to continue on her death. The annuity would be higher than the £3,132 per year with 100% continuing her death, but still lower than the £3652 per year without any continuing payments on her death.

Guarantee period and value protection

Guarantee period – One of the obvious concerns about an annuity purchase is what happens if you die too soon. This is especially important if you have not selected a joint life annuity. Since 2015 there has been no maximum guaranteed period; however, most insurers cap this at 30 years. The most common guarantee periods are 5 and 10 years.

The guarantee period is a length of time which the insurer guarantees to pay the income even if you die sooner. Usually, this guarantee period is paid out as a lump sum rather than an income.

A guarantee period can be combined with a joint life annuity.

As you would expect, the longer the guarantee period, the lower the annuity income.

Example

Jessie selects a joint life annuity with her husband. She asks for 50% of the annuity to continue to be payable upon her death. She also asks for a 5-year guarantee period.

If the original annuity is £4,000 per year and Jessie dies after three years. The insurance company will pay two more years of income at £4,000 per year. After this the joint life annuity continues to pay at 50% which results in £2,000 per year payable for the rest of Jessie's husband's life.

Value protection

This benefit ensures that when you die, your estate or beneficiaries receive a lump sum which is the difference between the amount you paid for your annuity and the gross income (that's the payments made before tax) you received before you died.

If you have already received more than you paid for your income, there will be no lump sum death benefit when you die.

This option, which is less commonly used than guarantee period, is also known as 'value protection' or 'capital protection'.

Value protection and guarantee periods are designed primarily to ensure you get more value from the annuity purchase. They provide the peace of mind to know that should you die shortly after purchasing an annuity your beneficiaries can still benefit.

Indexation

A fixed retirement income (sometimes called a level annuity) means you'll get the same level of pension payments year after year for the rest of your life.

This means that over time you'll be able to buy less with your income as prices of things like food and energy go up (inflation).

However, a fixed retirement income generally starts off higher than an increasing retirement income bought with a pension pot of the same size.

To help protect your income from rising prices, you can choose an increasing retirement income. This is sometimes called an escalating annuity.

With increasing income, you have two choices:

- An income that goes up each year at a set rate – usually 3% or 5%.

- An income that's adjusted each year in line with inflation – index linked.

Example

Again, for consistency of comparison let's look at Jessie. In the first example she purchased an annuity of £3,652 based on £75,000 pension pot. The annuity was on a single life basis with no guarantee period or value protection.

What happens if we request that this payment rises each year by 3%?

Now, the best annuity income we can receive is £2,402.76 per year. This is a significant reduction of income. The income will now rise each year by 3% unlike the original quote where the income remained the same.

Quite often I am asked the question, 'Which is better value, level or increasing?'. Although it's a fair question, I think it's important to accept that your expenditure will increase. For many this simple fact is ignored, which has consequences.

The cost of living will rise and so too will your expenses. Should you not have an income that increases with inflation, you simply can't buy the same amount of goods; you have to cut back.

Example

If my total expenditure is £2,000 per month and the cost of living rises by 3%, the following year, to have exactly the same expenditure/lifestyle I need an income of £2,060 per month.

If I still have £2,000 per month of income, I need to cut back £60 per month on my spending. If this continues over a long period of time, the impact on your lifestyle would be significant.

Ensuring your retirement plan takes account of inflation is a vital part of the overall planning.

Now let's consider the value question: what age do I need to live so that the increasing income becomes a 'better deal'?

According to my calculations in this example you would begin to get a higher income using the increasing annuity option from aged 80 onward. This is based on Jessie aged 65 having a level annuity of £3,652 per annum or an annuity increasing by 3% per annum starting at £2,402 per annum.

Another interesting statistic in this example is that you need to live until 92 if you choose the increasing annuity to have earned more in total income. This is due to the years between 65 and 80 when the income is lower from the increasing annuity. It then takes from years 80 to 92 of the now higher increasing income to compensate.

If you are unsure about this option, or indeed these example calculations, it is best to seek professional financial planning advice.

Disclosing your health

When purchasing an annuity, your health and lifestyle will be the main factors in deciding the level of annuity payments. If these factors are poor, there is an increased likelihood of you living a shorter life than the average person.

An enhanced annuity is the term for the higher rate for someone who has certain health problems or lifestyle choices which could reduce life expectancy. An example would be a heavy smoker or someone obese.

An impaired life annuity applies a similar principle, but in this case the higher annuity rates are due to confirmed medical conditions which would reduce life expectancy. An example would be someone who has had multiple heart attacks.

When applying for an annuity, the rate offered, particularly on impaired life annuities, depends on your medical information, plus, potentially, further information from your GP.

Temporary annuity

Another form of annuity is known as temporary. This pays a fixed income for a term rather than the whole of your life.

This can be useful for a situation where perhaps your expenditure needs are significantly higher for a limited period of time.

Example

Joe needs £4,000 per month of income. This will reduce in five years when his children are all through university. At this point his expenditure will be £2,000 per month. Joe could use some of his defined contribution pension to buy a temporary annuity of £2,000 per month for the next five years.

The cost of a temporary annuity is significantly less than a lifetime annuity as it's only payable for a fixed term. The insurance company have certainty that the payment will stop at this point. The longer the payment term the more expensive the temporary annuity becomes.

It Pays to Shop Around

In 1975 the open market option (OMO) was introduced for pensions. [39] Prior to this, when anyone approached retirement, they were always given an annuity by the pension provider who held their pension pot.

Because annuity purchase for many was the only option, the introduction of the open market option was designed to ensure retirees got a fair deal. The idea being that rather than having to accept the annuity offered by your pension provider, you could shop around to get a better offer.

The term OMO has become a campaign lead by the pensions industry to promote the idea that shopping around for your annuity can lead to a better deal. Once an annuity is purchased it can't be changed so it's important to get this deal right first time.

A significant percentage of people still don't shop around before purchasing an annuity. These individuals miss out a higher level of income in exchange for their capital. Like any purchase you are likely to have made in your lifetime, sometimes you can get the same item for less by going elsewhere. Some insurers are making more profit on the annuity purchase than others. It does pay to shop around.

Another reason for using the open market option is in relation to impaired and enhanced annuities. As previously discussed, due to disclosures around your health and lifestyle these can offer a higher income payment. The default annuity quote from your pension provider will not make allowances for any of these potential conditions, resulting in less income being offered.

We have considered who an annuity may suit and the options available when purchasing one. Let's now summarise by considering the advantages and disadvantages of a purchase.

Advantages

- Annuities provide certainty as the income can never decrease.

- Income is paid for life (unless a temporary annuity).

- No risk to your income.

- You can provide income for others after your death by including a joint life option.

- You can protect your income against inflation by including indexation.

Disadvantages

- No benefits are payable on death unless you select a joint life annuity, or include a guarantee period or value protection.

- The annuity is inflexible – you can't change it as all decisions are taken at the outset.

- Based on the timing of your annuity purchase, the rates aren't always the best value, this is the case today compared to historical rates.

- The insurance company benefits from all future returns on the capital, you don't. If the annuity rate is around 4–5% retirees often feel they could achieve this return through investing and keep full control of the capital themselves.

- You lose ownership and the ability to access the underlying funds.

- Annuity income is treated as taxable income & subject to income tax.

Pension withdrawals

It is widely agreed by pension experts that it's best to ensure you have guaranteed secure income for life to cover your essential expenditure. For any of your defined contribution pot that is not used to secure an annuity, these funds remain invested in the pension. Like any investment, no matter how cautious, it can fluctuate in value. These potential fluctuations could impact the amount of income you can receive.

For this reason, it's important that you have an underlying income that pays your main household bills.

For those who can cover their basic fixed expenditure with guaranteed income, they could consider alternative strategies for meeting discretionary expenditure.

There are several strategies when withdrawing from your pension pot. The underlying principle of each is the same. Your money remains invested and how much you receive over your lifetime depends on the performance of the investments within the pension pot.

The main strategies used to withdraw money from your pension pot are known as 'Drawdown' and 'Uncrystallised Fund Pension Lump Sum' (UFPLS). Deciding on which strategy is best depends on how much (if any) lump sum of capital you require and your individual tax position.

Drawdown v UFPLS

Under a drawdown arrangement you are taking the maximum tax-free lump sum at the outset. The remaining pension funds continue to be invested.

Any further withdrawals will be added to your income for the year and taxed in the normal way.

Under an UFPLS option the tax-free lump sum is not solely withdrawn. Instead, a cash sum is taken from the pension pot. The first 25% will be tax-free and the rest will be taxed at your appropriate tax rate. This option was introduced from April 2015 as part of the cash option for withdrawing your pension.

You can also move your pension pot gradually into income drawdown or UFPLS. This is known as a phased retirement.

Example

Bob and Kerry, both aged 60, have retired. They each have a pension pot of £100,000. Bob chooses a drawdown option. He takes his 25% tax-free lump sum of £25,000 and buys a car. The remaining £75,000 he takes a regular income of £2,500 gross each year. He hopes that the pension continues to be invested successfully to generate enough return to preserve the value of his pension.

Each £2,500 annual income is added to his other pension income. As Bob's defined benefit pension is £40,000, he is a basic rate taxpayer. Therefore, the £2,500 is within the basic rate tax band (£12,500 – £50,000) and Bob pays 20% tax on this annual withdrawal. After tax Bob is left with £2,000 each year.

If Bob only needed £12,500 for his new car and an income of £1,250 gross each year, he could have used a phased drawdown. In this situation, 50% of his pension fund would be 'crystallised'. The remaining £50,000 would be classed as an 'uncrystallised' pension pot. From the £50,000 of crystallised funds Bob takes the maximum tax-free lump sum of £12,500. He then withdraws £1,250 per year from the remaining £37,500 crystallised pension pot.

Later, Bob can still take 25% as a tax-free lump sum from the remaining uncrystallised pension pot.

Kerry does not have any planned expenditure. Her only other income is a small company pension of £4,000 per year. She chooses a phased UFPLS option. She withdraws £10,000 from her pension pot – this becomes 'crystallised'; the remaining £90,000 is 'uncrystallised'.

Of this withdrawal £2,500 is tax free; this represents 25% of the withdrawal. The remaining £7,500 is treated as taxable income and added to Kerry's pension. As the combined pension and taxable withdrawal (£4000 + £7500) is less than the personal allowance of £12,500, Kerry has no tax to pay on this withdrawal.

Kerry continues to take a £10,000 withdrawal each year from the remaining pension pot until the pension fund is depleted.

Kerry could have simply taken the entire pension pot of £100,000 as a lump sum. £25,000 would be tax free; the balance of £75,000 would be added to her other income of £4,000, giving her a taxable income of £79,000.

However, large withdrawals like this would push Kerry into the higher tax band and a portion of her withdrawal would be taxed at 40%.

The main advantages of pension withdrawals are as follows:

- The ability to have a flexible income

We have discussed how your expenditure needs can change as you age. For a significant portion of retirees, the later part of our retirement is not as active, with a reduction in spending. For this reason, rather than try to spread out a lump sum of capital evenly over a lifetime, some choose to spend a greater portion in the younger years.

Example

Margaret's income is made up of a state and defined benefit pension which pay an income of £2,000 per month. This covers all her living costs, with the exception of her holidays. She has just retired having reached age 65.

She has a pension pot valued at £100,000.

Margaret's mum passed away a few years ago; she was 100 years old. Margaret is hopeful she will live to the same age. If she does, this means Margaret would live another 35 years.

If Margaret spent the £100,000 over the 35 years this would give her £2,857 per year to spend on holidays. For simplicity I have not taken into consideration any investment growth, tax or inflation.

Margaret feels this would be enough to cover her basic holidays to Spain each year. However, reflecting back on her mum's life, although she lived to 100 Margaret recalls she stopped travelling abroad when she was 85, preferring to stay at home and take days trips out with the grandchildren.

For this reason, Margaret has decided to rethink her strategy. She does not know what her health will be like at 85, if she does live that long. However, if she is like her mum, she may even have the health and appetite to travel beyond age 85. For this reason, she would like to retain £20,000 of her pension pot at age 85.

The remaining £80,000 she would like to spend on holidays between now and then. This £80,000 divided over a 20-year period means she can spend £4,000 on holidays each year.

She has decided she would like to take advantage of the extra £1,143 per year (£4,000 – £2857) and holiday in Dubai. She has more income to afford this holiday and she feels more than comfortable with the longer flight. She acknowledges that as she gets older, she may find this flight too long.

At 85 she'll have £20,000 remaining. Should she be fortunate enough to be in the position of continuing her holidays abroad for a further 10 years, she would have £2,000 per year to spend. This would mean reducing the frequency of

AN EXPERT GUIDE TO RETIREMENT

her holidays. Margaret is happy to accept this trade off as she feels it's unlikely she would holiday beyond 85 and prefers more luxurious holidays in the earlier part of her retirement while she knows she will enjoy them.

Should Margaret choose, she could take a, world cruise to celebrate her 70th birthday costing an additional £10,000. The trade-off being less available capital after 85. An annuity purchase would not allow this type of flexibility; a pension withdrawals strategy does.

- Legacy payments

Except for an annuity that provides value protection, any other type of annuity has a limitation on the death benefits payable to your family. Annuities can include guarantee periods that ensure the payments are paid for a fixed term even if you pass away earlier. In addition, some annuities will pay a continuing income to your spouse/civil partner. However, these will stop upon death of your spouse/civil partner.

With any form of pension withdrawal, the value of the funds remaining in the pension pot can pass to your family. We will cover the taxation and options open to your family in more detail later. However, in principle a pension pot being used for regular withdrawals can provide a legacy to your family. Upon death your beneficiaries can use the capital for whatever purpose they choose.

Example

Paula aged 65 lives with her only son Josh, 23. Josh's father sadly passed away 10 years ago. Paula has retired with a combined income from her state pension and defined benefit scheme of £2,500 per month.

Paula has a pension pot valued at £75,000. She does not need this to pay her regular bills but will use it to fund holidays. Paula had considered using this pension pot to purchase an annuity. She was quoted £3,652 per year for life without any increase. This would cease on her death.

As Paula is widowed, she has no spouse to include as a joint life to ensure the annuity would continue on her death. She has considered the options of including a guarantee period, value protection or adding Josh as a joint life. However, all of the options considerably reduce the amount of income payable each year. Paula has three main objectives.

1. Have a regular income to fund holidays if possible. Paula is prepared to accept that should the pension pot not perform well this could reduce her holiday budget.

2. Ensure she gets value out of this pension pot as she has worked hard throughout her life to accumulate this money. Paula has a friend who bought an annuity and died after one year. She felt this was a waste of money as her friend had got so little out of the pot.

3. Leave the maximum legacy possible to Josh.

Paula instead decides to leave the pension pot invested. She hopes it will earn a 4% return on average each year as she is a fairly cautious investor. This average return would pay her an income of £3,000 per year (£75,000 x 4%). Although this is less than the £3,652 single annuity, it is greater than the alternative annuity quotations which included the long-term protection to the payments.

Paula has the peace of mind to know that upon her death, Josh can inherit the full value of the pension pot and spend this money in whatever way he feels best.

- The ability to spend the pension pot on a larger purchase

When a generous defined benefit pension is combined with a state pension, this can provide enough income for some. If this is enough income, the value of the pension pot can be used to fund a large purchase. This situation usually occurs when no other funds are accessible through personal savings and investments outside of the pension pot.

It is important to highlight that withdrawing money from your pension beyond the tax-free lump sum is taxable. Therefore, care needs to be taken to ensure you don't pay excessive amounts of income tax unnecessarily.

Example

Ciaran has reached 60. He has decided to retire and has more than enough pension income from his defined benefit pension of £3,800 per month before tax (£44,400 per year). This income will be further increased when he reaches his state pension at 67. His state pension is projected to be £179.60 per week (£9,339.20 per year).

Ciaran has £30,000 of cash in his savings but he wants to keep this for emergency purposes. He would like to purchase a caravan in Portrush to enjoy throughout his retirement. The cost of this is £40,000. Ciaran does not want to use any of his income to finance the caravan as he wants this to fund his lifestyle. He also does not like the idea of borrowing money to purchase a caravan.

Ciaran does hold a pension fund worth £40,000. He would like to use this to fund the purchase. Let's consider how he could do this.

Ciaran withdraws the pension pot with one full withdrawal:

Ciaran would be entitled to 25% of the fund tax free. Therefore, £10,000 of the fund would be tax free. The remaining £30,000 would be treated as income for income tax purposes.

As Ciaran's pension income is £44,400, this £30,000 withdrawal would increase his taxable income to £74,400.

Ciaran has used his personal allowance of £12,500 through his pension income. Ciaran can earn £37,500 and pay basic rate income tax at 20%. Ciaran's pension income of £44,400 is using up not only the personal allowance but £31,900 of the basic rate tax band (£44,400 less £12,500 = £31,900)

Ciaran can earn an additional £5,600 of income at a 20% tax rate (£37,500 less £31,900). Any income above this figure will pay 40% tax.

By withdrawing these pension funds, the £30,000 of taxable income will suffer tax as follows:

£5,600 X 20% = £1,120

£24,400 (£30,000 less £5,600) X 40% = £9,760

Total tax payable £ 10,880

Therefore, although Ciaran can withdraw his £40,000 to fund the caravan purchase, he will only receive £29,120. (£40,000 less £10,880 income tax)

Ciaran withdraws his tax-free lump sum immediately and the balance gradually.

Ciaran would be entitled to 25% of the fund tax free. Therefore £10,000 of the fund would be tax free. The remaining £30,000 would be treated as income for income tax purposes.

Ciaran has used his personal allowance of £12,500 through his pension income. Ciaran can earn another £37,500 and pay basic rate income tax at 20%. Ciaran's pension income of £44,400 is using up not only the personal allowance but £31,900 of the basic rate tax band (£44,400 less £12,500 = £31,900)

Ciaran can earn an additional £5,600 of income at a 20% tax rate (£37,500 less £31,900). Any income above this figure will pay 40% tax.

Ciaran therefore withdraws £5,600 per year for 5 years totalling £28,000 (£5,600 x 5). Each would suffer 20% tax.

£5,600 x 20% = £1,120 x 5 years = £5,600 income tax.

On the 6th year the pension would now hold £2000 (£30,000 initially less £28,000 withdrawn).

This remaining £2,000 is now withdrawn and taxed at 20% = £400 tax.

The total tax payable is £6,000 (£5,600 years 1–5 and £400 in year 6).

This is £4,880 less tax than option 1 when all the money was taken out in one withdrawal.

In both examples Ciaran will still need to use some of his emergency funds to purchase a caravan. However, by phasing the withdrawal over six years he pays much less in tax. Ciaran would need to consider the option of paying for the caravan over six years.

He would of course, potentially, to pay interest on the finance to purchase the caravan. The cost of this finance would need to be balanced against the potential tax saving of withdrawing the money over the 6-year term.

For illustration purposes we have frozen the pension value, tax rates and tax bands, it is unlikely in the real world that these would not change.

In this example it's also worth highlighting that in seven years Ciaran would begin to receive his state pension. From this point on he is likely to pay higher rate tax as this combined with his defined benefit scheme will use up all of his basic rate tax band (£9,339 state pension plus £44,400 defined benefit = £53,739).

For this reason, if Ciaran is going to consider withdrawing from the pension each year he should not delay, as any withdrawals once in receipt of his state pension would be subject to 40% income tax rather than 20% basic rate.

Clearly this is a more complicated discussion and tax calculation. It would be advisable to seek advice from a regulated financial planner.

So having considered the advantages of a pension withdrawal strategy, let's look at the main disadvantages.

- It's healthy to emphasise that withdrawing from your pension carries risks.

Firstly, the pension fund itself will carry charges. If the pension fund has no actual growth, then the value will reduce simply through the charges incurred by the pension provider.

To achieve any growth in the pension, to at least offset against the charges, the fund needs to be invested. Any investment can fall as well as rise in value. Therefore, even a cautiously invested pension pot could result in a loss of capital.

If you plan to withdraw from the pension but preserve the value of the pot, perhaps to one day pass on as a legacy. You need to consider that the growth must not only cover the charges of the pension but the level of withdrawals you're taking.

If your aim is to leave a legacy on death, the value of this legacy will reduce unless you ensure the pension pot grows in line with inflation.

A pension fund withdrawal strategy can be complex. It is likely regular financial advice will be required, and this is an additional layer of charges that the fund needs to cover.

Example

Although Gilbert has retired, he has decided to leave his pension invested. He sees this as a legacy for his children upon his death. The value of the pension pot is £100,000. His pension provider charges 0.5% per year as an annual management fee. In addition, Gilbert takes £1,000 per year to pay his rates bill. This represents 1% of the pension value. Gilbert has a regular review with his financial planner who charges 1% per year.

If Gilbert's pension grows by 2.5% (£2,500) every year this would cover the annual management charge (£500), the £1,000 withdrawal and the £1000 financial planner's fee.

Gilbert's aim is to leave the £100,000 legacy to his family and ensure this increases with inflation. A 2.5% return will mean the value of the pension will not grow. If average annual inflation is 2.5% per year over a 27-year period. The value of the £100,000 will now amount to £50,481. [40]

Therefore, the growth in the pension needs to be 5% to cover the costs and ensure the value keeps pace with 2.5% annual inflation.

The greater the return required, the more volatility the retiree will experience and indeed need to accept. Even if this volatility is accepted as a trade-off for the potential return required, there is no guarantee that the return will be achieved.

Should the pension pot not generate enough return, the value of the fund will reduce accordingly. For this reason, a pension withdrawal strategy should not be considered for essential expenditure. This is known as a 'safety first' strategy.

- Money Purchase Annual Allowance (MPAA)

A pension is recognised as an extremely tax efficient way to save for your future. Due to the tax benefits a pension offers, HMRC have some restrictions in the amount of tax relief you can claim through payment into your pension. When you withdraw from your pension for the first time any amount above the 25% tax-free lump sum, you trigger this restricted allowance.

This restriction prevents you from claiming tax relief on any more than £4000 per year of future pension contributions. This is a sizeable reduction from the standard annual allowance figure currently £40,000.

For this reason, anyone who is considering withdrawing from the taxable part of their pension part needs to consider how this might impact any existing pension contributions they make. Equally, consideration should be given to the impact this could have on any future planned pension contributions.

This is commonly a problem we encounter for some retirees wanting to access pension benefits but who continue to work. Perhaps their existing pension receives contributions in excess of £10,000. Should this be the case and the MPAA is triggered, this contribution is now £6,000 above the permitted amount.

If the MPAA is triggered this will result in a tax charge for the pension member, which can come as a surprise. Calculating the maximum you can pay into a pension can be complicated. If you have any doubt on this matter, you should speak to a regulated financial planner.

- Taxation

In the previous example with Ciaran's caravan purchase, we highlighted how not planning your pension withdrawals can lead to a higher income tax liability.

In addition, when you are making a pension withdrawal, unless the pension provider holds an up-to-date code, most withdrawals will incur the emergency tax code. This will result in an overpayment of tax for most when making their first taxable pension withdrawal.

This overpayment will need to be reclaimed from HMRC.

Deciding which company should manage your pension

Once you have decided on how best to draw benefits from your pension, you need to establish if your pension provider can facilitate this.

With the introduction of pension freedoms, HMRC permitted a more flexible approach to how benefits are withdrawn from your pension. Some pension providers have updated their contract terms and conditions to reflect these freedoms. However, a number of pensions don't facilitate some of these new options such as drawdown or UFPLS.

Even if your existing pension provider does facilitate your preferred pension withdrawal strategy, it's important to compare other pension options available. Just like annuities it pays to shop around.

If using drawdown or UFPLS to withdraw from your pension, charges, choice of funds, service and flexibility might vary from one provider to another.

Comparing pension options can be difficult but a financial planner can do this for you. It's the planner's role to recommend the product that is most suited to your needs and circumstances.

We have listed an 8-step checklist to consider when deciding if your pensions are appropriately invested:

1. Establish what pensions you hold

In the previous chapter if you have completed question 6 this will already be done. It's amazing the number of clients I have met over the years who have lost or forgotten about an old pension. Try to cross reference your career history with your pension schemes. Look out for periods of longer employment without any pension provision. If you have any gaps you can't account for, contact the pensions department of the employer in question. It is useful to know your address at the time employment if you have since moved house.

Even if an old employer does not exist, in most cases it does not mean your pension entitlement is gone. If you're struggling to locate a pension arrangement, try the government's pension tracing service. When this service was launched in 2016 there was an estimated £400 million in unclaimed pension savings. With an average of 11 jobs during our working life it's easy to see how this could happen. The database enables a search of over 320,000 pensions. [41]

https://www.gov.uk/find-pension-contact-details

If this does not yield any results you could contact the Pension Protection Fund. They look after defined benefit pension arrangements where the sponsoring employer has become insolvent.

https://www.ppf.co.uk/

Another source of information about potentially forgotten defined benefit pension schemes is the National Insurance Contribution Office. They can help if your pension was contracted out of National Insurance, which means that NI contributions were diverted out to the pension scheme, reducing your entitlement to additional state pension benefits such as state-earnings-related pensions (SERPS). If in any doubt, you should try this service anyway.

2. Establish the main features and benefits of your defined contribution pensions

This is vital, as failure to get this right can mean missing out on valuable benefits. Alternatively, continuing with a pension that is underperforming or too expensive can significantly reduce the benefits you receive.

I must stress this is a complicated area that requires great care. If you're unsure about evaluating your pension at this point, it's best to get advice from a suitably qualified financial planner. Although by no means an exhaustive list, here are some of the key questions you need to answer regarding your pension:

- List all the charges applied to your pension.

- Are there any penalties should you transfer or access your benefits?

- What investment funds does your pension invest in?

- What other alternative investment funds does the pension have available? If alternatives exist, is there any cost to switch your fund?

- Establish if drawdown or UFPLS is an option and if so, do any additional costs apply?

- Does the pension have a Guaranteed Annuity Rate or Guaranteed Growth Rate?

- How much of a tax-free lump sum are you entitled to as some arrangements can offer more than the normal 25%?

3. Decide how you want your pension money invested

4. Summarise your overall pension needs

Firstly, you should know which withdrawal strategy you wish to apply (drawdown or UFPLS). Secondly, your investment objectives should clearly define how much growth you expect the pension to achieve. This target level of growth should not only be realistic but also accepting of the likely associated volatility that comes with it. Remember, the higher the future growth, the more day-to-day volatility you're likely to experience.

You will certainly want a reputable and reliable pension provider. Fees should be set at a reasonable level in comparison to the wider market. Some retirees search for the cheapest pension fees possible. I must warn against this approach. One pension arrangement being cheaper than the other does not guarantee a successful investment outcome. Having said that, fees should not be excessive.

You also need to consider how you plan to interact with the pension provider. Some retirees will want online access to their pension portfolio whilst others will want more support, perhaps through a telephone service. For those using a financial planner this area won't carry as much importance, as the planner will be their regular point of contact.

5. Establish how closely your existing pension arrangement meets your needs

Consider how closely your pension covers your needs (point 4). List any areas where it falls short. In addition, consider what features of the existing pension could benefit you. Could any of these benefits be lost if the pension is changed?

6. Consider alternative pension providers that meet your needs

Some of the main reasons we have switched a pension for a retiree are listed below. It can take an enormous amount of time to research the pension market and understand what is available. When considering alternative providers, we suggest dividing your research into two sections: firstly, researching the pension providers; and secondly, researching investment funds – as your preferred investment funds need to be available within your selected pension provider.

As a firm of advisors, we use various systems to support you in this research, and we pay to use the support of specialist research companies who have extra knowledge within specific areas, so we can tailor recommendations to your specific needs.

When comparing providers, pay particular attention to the following:

- Facilitation of your preferred withdrawal strategy (drawdown or UFPLS)

- Financial strength of the organisation

- Level of customer service, particularly how you can contact and discuss queries with them

- All potential charges you may incur

Listing all the areas to consider before choosing an appropriate investment strategy could require a book in itself. Having answered question 3 and now knowing how you want your pension money invested, consider the following:

- Past and likely future performance of the funds

- Charges for management of the fund

- Reputation and history of the fund management company

- Is the fund available with your preferred pension provider?

7. Compare your pension to the alternatives

At this point you should know what benefits your existing pension contract holds. You need to weigh up the benefits of your existing pension compared to others available in the wider market.

Consider specifically what benefits would be lost should you switch your pension to a new provider. Additionally, what charges, if any, would you incur should you move your pension to a new arrangement. These potential negatives need to be weighed up against benefits.

For example, perhaps an alternative pension offers access to an investment fund that your existing pension arrangement does not offer. If this alternative fund has historically delivered a higher return, the following questions need to be considered:

- Is the new pension likely to yield a higher return that the old scheme?

- Does this extra return outweigh the costs of making the change?

- How likely is the new fund to continue generating higher returns?

In more recent times retirees are often wanting to take advantage of a drawdown arrangement and finding their existing pension does not offer this option. Although they may pay some costs to make a change, the benefits of using the drawdown may outweigh the costs.

Everyone's circumstances are different based on what pension pots they hold and their objectives. A balanced approach to your decision making at this point is important to ensure the right decision is taken.

8. Implement any changes

Moving your pension to a new provider is often not a straightforward process. It isn't just writing to the new firm and requesting a transfer. You can expect a switch of pensions to take some weeks. Your new chosen pension should firstly be set up to receive the funds from the old provider.

Some providers are likely to check that you know what you are doing. They may ask if you have received advice or ask you to certify that you're aware of the risks involved in managing your investment. They will normally require written instruction in the post from you.

Once your request has been sent you should monitor progress. This process involves your existing pension provider communicating with the new provider. Whilst some pension providers provide an excellent service others can be difficult to deal with at this point.

The key to implementing any change of pension is regular communication with both the new and existing pension provider. Each provider will have its own paperwork and processes to follow. I have experienced some pensions being switched within a few weeks to other cases that took over three months. For anyone instructing a financial planner, you should be spared the pain of this process as your planner can take care of this on your behalf.

Lifetime allowance for pension savings

The lifetime allowance is a limit on the value of pay-outs from your pension schemes – whether lump sums or retirement income – that can be made without triggering an extra tax charge. This guide explains the rules and how to protect your allowance.

- How much is the lifetime allowance?
- Charges if you exceed the lifetime allowance
- Individual Protection 2016
- Fixed Protection 2016

How much is the lifetime allowance?:

The lifetime allowance for most people is £1,073,100 in the tax year 2021–22.

It applies to the total of all the pensions you have, including the value of pensions promised through any defined benefit schemes you belong to, but excluding your State Pension.

Working out if this applies to you:

Every time a pay-out from your pension schemes starts, its value is compared against your remaining lifetime allowance to see if there is additional tax to pay.

You can work out whether you are likely to be affected by adding up the expected value of your pay-outs.

You work out the value of pensions differently depending on the type of scheme you are in:

1. For defined contribution pension schemes, including all personal pensions, the value of your benefits will be the value of your pension pot used to fund your retirement income and any lump sum.
2. For defined benefit pension schemes, you calculate the total value by multiplying your expected annual pension by 20. In addition, you need to add to this the amount of any tax-free cash lump sum if it is additional to the pension. In many schemes, you would only get a lump sum by giving up some pension, in which case the value of the full pension captures the full value of your pay-outs. So, you are likely to be affected by the lifetime allowance in 2021–22 if you are on track for a final salary pension (with no separate lump sum) of more than £53,655 a year.

Note that certain tax-free lump sum benefits paid out to your survivors if you die before age 75 also use up lifetime allowance.

Whenever you start taking money from your pension, a statement from your scheme should tell you how much of your lifetime allowance you are using up.

Whether or not you take money from your pension, a check will be made once you reach the age of 75 against any unused funds or undrawn entitlements.

Charges if you exceed the lifetime allowance:

If the cumulative value of the pay-outs from your pension pots, including the value of the pay-outs from any defined benefit schemes, exceeds the lifetime allowance, there will be tax on the excess – called the lifetime allowance charge.

The way the charge applies depends on whether you receive the money from your pension as a lump sum or as part of regular retirement income.

Lump sums

Any amount over your lifetime allowance that you take as a lump sum is taxed at 55%.

Your pension scheme administrator should deduct the tax and pay it over to HMRC, paying the balance to you.

Income

Any amount over your lifetime allowance that you take as a regular retirement income – for instance by buying an annuity – attracts a lifetime allowance charge of 25%.

This is on top of any tax payable on the income in the usual way.

For defined contribution pension schemes, your pension scheme administrator should pay the 25% tax to HMRC out of your pension pot, leaving you with the remaining 75% to use towards your retirement income.

For example, suppose someone who pays tax at the higher rate had expected to get £1,000 a year as income but the 25% lifetime allowance charge reduced this to £750 a year.

After income tax at 40%, the person would be left with £450 a year.

This means the lifetime allowance charge and combined taxation have reduced the income by 55% – the same as the lifetime allowance charge had the benefits been taken as a lump sum instead of income.

For defined benefit pension schemes, your pension scheme might decide to pay the tax on your behalf and recover it from you by reducing your pension.

If you wish to avoid the lifetime allowance charge it's important to monitor the value of your pensions, and especially the value of changes to any defined benefit pensions as these can be surprisingly large.

You might also wish to consider applying for protection if your pension savings is expected to exceed the lifetime allowance threshold.

Protecting your lifetime allowance

There were and are schemes that allow you to protect your lifetime allowance.

You can check if you already have protection but you will need an account for HM Revenue and Customers (HMRC) online services.

If you don't have an account <u>you can create one</u>.

If your total pension savings exceeded £1 million on 5 April 2016 there are still two schemes you can apply for – <u>Individual Protection 2016 and Fixed Protection 2016</u>.

I would recommend speaking to your financial planner if these are issues that impact you.

Chapter 7

Options at retirement – part 3

"Foresight is not about predicting the future, it's about minimising surprise." Karl Schroeder

Hopefully the previous chapters have given you enough information to begin considering your own retirement strategy. Before making any major decisions on your future retirement, it's vital to consider how the world around us may change. Take a few minutes to reflect how much the world has changed over your lifetime. As an example, here are some changes since the turn of the millennium.

Internet usage – Google as a company were only 5 years old! Now, 4 billion people use the internet.

Smoking in restaurants – How many of us non-smokers remember coming home from a night out with clothes smelling of cigarette smoke?

Television – I remember Sky TV being a revolution. Now we watch programmes, sport and films, online via websites such as

Netflix and Amazon. Can you remember going to the video shop to rent a film?

Music – The CD replaced the vinyl many years ago. Now, who buys CDs? Streaming of music from sites such as Apple or Spotify continues to be the norm.

Holidays – Perhaps showing our age but going on holiday used to be a complete break from society. The only way to keep up to date with world affairs was the newspaper which usually was a day or two behind. Now, social media and the internet mean we generally don't have detachment from real life when we're on holiday unless we specifically choose to.

Telephone numbers – How many telephone numbers do you remember? In 1999 it would have been a lot more than today. The mobile phone has almost replaced the house phone and means we carry numbers in our phones, not in our memory.

Photographs – How many of us have a camera we use for photography? Most of us now use our phones to take pictures.

Undoubtably the world will continue to change throughout your retirement. Whilst many of these changes won't impact on you, some will. For this reason, it's important you consider what external factors may impact your retirement plan. Whilst it's impossible to predict the future, it's crucial your retirement plan factors in change.

Financial planners will refer to this as "What if?" scenarios.

For example, you may expect your savings to grow at 1% per year on average. However, what happens if this is not the case, and they grow at 0.5%?

Changes in your own lifestyle combined with the changes in the world mean it's vital your retirement plan is reviewed. Whilst an annuity is inflexible, anyone using a pension withdrawal strategy such as drawdown can completely change their strategy at a later date.

Future assumptions to consider in your retirement plan

Here we have listed the main assumptions you need to factor into your retirement plan. This is not an exhaustive list.

1. Inflation

Having completed an expenditure list both now and for later life, you should now have an accurate idea of how much money you will need each month. Let's consider the impact inflation could have on your required income.

Using the Candid Money inflation calculator, in 2000 if you had an income of £2,000 per month, by 2010 you would now need £2625.48 to be able to buy the same goods. This is based on an average inflation rate over this time of 2.8%. [42]

If we change the start year to 2005, review how this has changed to 2015. Over this period, you would need £2,696.69, due to average inflation of 3%. This change is fairly modest.

To show a more extreme change, imagine someone requiring £2,000 over a 10-year period beginning in 1970. By 1980 they would have required £7,214.77 which is an average annual increase of 13.7%!

It's impossible to predict what inflation will do over the course of your retirement. For this reason, you need to do the following:

- Take account of inflation when building your long-term retirement strategy.

- Consider how your strategy will play out should inflation be more or less than you expected.

- Review your plan regularly to sense check inflation levels against your predictions.

- Check your sources of guaranteed income and what inflationary increases will apply – if any.

2. National average earnings

Should part of your retirement plan include some form of continued income from employment, perhaps on a part-time basis, this income may increase in value.

- Consider by how much this income may increase during your retirement.

- Consider how your strategy will play out should your earnings be more or less than you expected.

- Review your plan regularly to sense check increases against your predictions.

3. Interest rates

Perhaps part of your retirement plan includes capital you wish to hold in cash-based savings. At the time of writing, interest rates are at a historic low 0.1%. This was not always the case.

On the 6th February 2000 the Bank of England increased the rate of interest to 6%. This fluctuated frequently to a low of 3.5% on 10th July 2003 and high of 5.75% on 5th July 2007.

From this point on rates declined rapidly with the 'credit crunch', reaching 0.5% in March 2009. This remained unchanged until 4th August 2016 during which they were further reduced to 0.25%. [43]

Choosing a predicted long-term rate of interest on your savings is difficult. Like all of these external factors, consider how your retirement plan should change if the interest rate differs.

4. Taxation

Some of your income will likely come from pensions. Changes to the rates of income tax and personal allowance (amount of income free from taxation) will impact your pension income.

In 1980, Margaret Thatcher, in her first budget, reduced the basic rate of income tax from 33% to 30%. [44]. Today, the basic rate of income tax is 20%. Income tax changes tend not to be drastic at each budget review; however, let's consider what such a difference in income tax rates would mean.

For the purposes of this example let's presume the personal allowance is £12,500 and the income is £30,000.

This would leave £17,500 of income taxable.

Should we apply today's rate of 20%, this results in £3,500 of income tax. (£17,500 x 20% = £3,500).

Should we apply the rate in 1980 of 33%, this changes the income tax to £5,775. (£17,500 x 33% = £5,775).

Therefore, you would lose £2,275 more in tax. Another way to look at this would be each month you would be £189.58 worse off.

Taxation can be a complicated area, particularly as some of your investments may pay capital gains tax and not income tax. Should you not be comfortable with this area, it would be best to seek advice from a suitably qualified financial planner.

As demonstrated, changes to income tax should be factored into your retirement plan to ensure your needs continue to be met should tax rates increase in future.

5. Investment returns

If some part of your portfolio is likely to remain invested in retirement, you will need to establish a long-term projected return. So how do we decide what is an appropriate rate of growth to forecast over the long term?

There have been several advisors who have written papers covering this area.

One of the earliest and most well-known is by William Bengen. This paper established a safe withdrawal rate from a simple equity bond-based investment portfolio. Using historical market data rather than averages, he established a safe withdrawal rate as a percentage of the initial portfolio adjusted for inflation each year. This rate is the highest that someone can withdraw without running out of money, over any 30-year period in history. This figure was calculated with the worst sequence of market returns and inflation over the last 100 years.

His figure was calculated at 4% and became known as the 4% rule. Many financial planners would agree this is too simple an approach. Firstly, not everyone will invest in a portfolio with a 60% equity and 40% bond split. The asset allocation within a portfolio is likely to be driven by how cautious or adventurous the retiree is with money. Indeed, the agreed investment strategy will also need to consider how much capacity for loss they can tolerate in falling market conditions.

The 4% rule also presumes that the individual is happy with the idea that the portfolio value could decrease throughout the 30-year period. Many retirees will want to leave a legacy to their family. This goal to leave a legacy will mean they need to balance the level of income from their pension pots to ensure their capital is not depleted beyond a level they feel is acceptable.

Lastly, as we have highlighted throughout this book, in our experience, spending patterns in retirement change.

The 4% rule ignores the idea that our expenditure will likely change as we age. The calculation assumes we will spend the same amount each year for the rest of our lives.

This method does not allow for sequencing risk, which is explained in the next few pages.

Within our practice we prefer to choose a bespoke investment projection for each retirement plan. This starts with a regular review of investment portfolios across a spectrum of risk profiles. Within each risk profile we consider the ideal weighted asset allocation mainly combining equities, bonds, cash, property and alternative assets.

Based on the asset allocation of each portfolio, from the lowest risk to the highest risk, we have agreed a long-term estimated rate of return.

We choose this long-term projection based on historic data which considers the long-term rates of return each asset class has produced. Our projections also need to consider how future returns may differ from the past. In addition, your projections need to allow for taxation and charges within the investment fund that will erode the real return.

Certain forces in recent times are driving returns lower than historical averages. Recent decades have witnessed slowing economic growth, falling inflation and lower interest rates. These forces lead to a lower projected future return.

One reason for lower economic growth is simply because it has been higher in the past. Many 'emerging financial markets' have caught up with their peers. Many technology gains have been made in recent times, an example being that the Apple iPhone 1 was a huge leap in technology. Whilst Apple continue to launch new phones, these have not revolutionised the market in the same way as the original.

Another reason to consider lower future investment returns is that globally the world population is 10 years older than over

50 years ago. An ageing population tends to reduce long-term economic growth.

Having decided on future rates of return for each investment portfolio, this can in turn be matched to your chosen investment strategy. Should you wish to ensure your retirement pot does not erode its capital value, any projected income should not outstrip this projected return.

Many retirees don't mind the idea of eroding capital and are happy to see the value of the retirement pot fall through time. Should this be the case, a higher income can be taken than the projected return. It is stating the obvious but once a retiree begins withdrawing consistently more from the retirement pot than the rate of return, the long-term implications need to be considered.

Eventually the pot of money will run down and therefore cashflow modelling and considerations for these long-term assumptions become vital. Should the portfolio be a 60/40 equity bond split, and the level of income be consistent over 30 years, then perhaps the 4% rule could be applied in this scenario. Should this not be the case, the rate of return needs to be different. We struggle to see how a retirement plan in this situation can be effective without using some cashflow modelling software and reviewing this regularly.

Cashflow modelling

Cashflow modelling is the process that financial planners use to show the long-term impact of the decisions we take today. A retirement strategy that appears to work based on your circumstances today may not work in future.

I enjoyed Maths at school. However, I would not like to manually calculate each year over a 30-year period how I will be financially impacted by different factors such as taxation, interest rates or investment returns changing.

These calculations would be further complicated when you acknowledge that each of your forecasted assumptions could turn out to be different.

For example, let's consider you have calculated the impact of inflation at 2.5% over 30 years on your retirement plan. You want to consider how this would change if inflation was 1% and 4%? This would require a lot more calculations.

Now imagine trying to do this by forecasting variations to multiple long-term factors! My head begins to spin just thinking about it.

Most financial planners today will use cashflow modelling software that takes away all these calculations. By inputting an accurate picture of your circumstances today, the software will project the impact these factors will have on your retirement plan.

The projections you input, such as inflation rates, can be changed very easily and in turn the software will recalculate the impact on your plan.

It's not only the world around us which changes; we change as well. What you want to spend money on today is likely to change over time. Your health may change, having an impact on how long you may be around, and as such on your expenditure needs.

Countless numbers of clients would contact us and ask the "What if I…" question.

Typical reasons for "What if?" include gifting money to the children, paying for an operation. or possibly buying a holiday home.

When we get this question, we can easily alter the cashflow planning software and highlight how this change in your retirement plan will impact you.

Below we have taken a screen shot of a typical cashflow modelling chart. This shows a projection of what we have calculated will happen to a client's assets over time. This forecast is showing very little change to their wealth throughout their lifetime. This is based on spending £27,600 per year. Underpinning this will be a lot of information on their current assets, income and expenditure, both now and in future. In addition, assumptions will have been agreed around all the external factors we have explained, such as inflation. In this case we used an inflation rate of 2.5%.

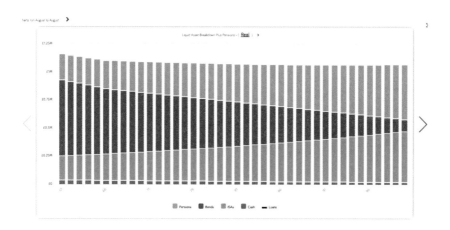

Now look at how this chart alters when we increase the expenditure to £50,000 per year and inflation to 5%. From age 83 this individual runs out of money.

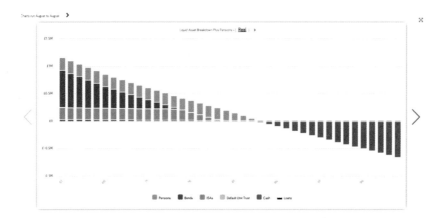

Stress testing

Once we have built a financial plan and considered the impact of these assumptions varying, we can take this a step further. This step considers the impact of more catastrophic events in your plan.

1. Death

What happens to your spouse or partner's income should one of you die? Can the other survive financially from this point on? Although the expenses may be projected to decrease, do they still have the income to live out their required lifestyle? Perhaps this could highlight a need for life insurance.

2. Long-term care

Should either you or your partner/spouse fall ill and no longer be able to live at home, what impact would the cost of care home fees have on the long-term plan?

As mentioned in a previous chapter, the LaingBuisson Care of Older People Report 2019 estimates the cost of residential care in Northern Ireland to be £534 per week and nursing care to be £691 per week.

3. Market crash events

Whilst you may have carefully taken the time to review the long-term projected return your portfolio could achieve, it's unlikely this rate of return will play out year on year. In fact, it's unlikely you will see any years match the exact predicted future rate. What's likely to play out is a variation of returns. Over the long term the hope would be that the average of each year's return will match your long-term prediction.

History would suggest that within the long-term average some years will see exceptional levels of growth while other years painful lows.

It's important to stress test what impact these 'crash events' would have on your day-to-day financial plan. In addition, mathematics starts to play a part on the impact this can have on your retirement plan. Although the average rate of return may meet your long-term average projection, the order and way these returns play out can have an impact on your capital in retirement.

4. Sequence risk

Poor returns in early retirement can create major damage to the level of income you receive throughout the rest of your life. This concept is not measuring how much your capital can fluctuate in value throughout retirement. Sequence risk looks at how the overall value of your pension pots can change depending on the years each return is applied.

These charts below from Brooks Macdonald summarise this well. [45]

Both these charts show a £100,000 portfolio invested over 35 years. It highlights why you should consider the impact of variable returns, particularly incorporating heavy losses in the early part of your retirement.

This first chart has no withdrawals and shows the returns with varying returns.

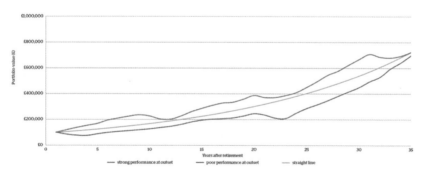

For illustrative purposes only. Source: Brooks Macdonald, September 2018.

- The reason that the 'poor performance at outset' line recovers over time is because when markets are weak, the portfolio is able to reinvest at lower prices (because no withdrawals are being made in this example).

- Portfolio value therefore has the ability to recover and return to the long-term average over time.

This chart includes withdrawals of £5,000 per annum with the same returns as chart 1.

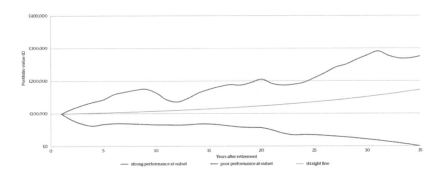

For illustrative purposes only. Source: Brooks Macdonald, September 2018.

- If the portfolio enjoys good performance at outset, portfolio growth is able to overcome the amount of income being withdrawn, and portfolio value increases over 35 years.

- If the portfolio suffers from weak returns at the outset and £5,000 of income has been withdrawn every year, the portfolio never has enough time to recover those initial losses.

When is sequencing risk at its highest?

- At the start of an investor's decumulation phase (i.e. when they begin to rely on their portfolio for income)

- Having saved up for retirement during their lifetime, at this point both the investor's portfolio value and the timeframe over which income is required are at their highest

Summary

- Sequencing risk is the risk created by the combination of the 'sequence' in which returns are generated and the withdrawals made from a portfolio

- It affects investors making withdrawals from their portfolio, and particularly those in the 'decumulation' or retirement phase

- Sequencing risk is at its highest in the earliest years of decumulation, when both portfolio value and the time horizon are at their greatest

Which pot should you withdraw money from?

An area of expertise that can add significant value to your wealth is knowing which of your pensions and investments is best to access.

A pension's purpose is as a tax efficient vehicle to build up capital which supports your retirement.

In years gone by, logically, retirees have used pensions as the main method to support their income in retirement. However, purely from a taxation point of view this is not always a good idea.

Let's consider the area of inheritance tax. Inheritance tax is a taxation that is sometimes payable on your estate should you pass away with assets above a certain limit. The rate of inheritance tax is normally 40%.

Should a retiree have retirement pots built up within a pension and perhaps a savings account, on death the funds within the pension are likely to be free from inheritance tax, whilst the funds in the savings account would be included in the estate for inheritance tax purposes.

If circumstances allowed, and reducing inheritance tax is a priority for the retiree, perhaps it would be best to not withdraw from the pension and lean more heavily on the savings account.

If reducing income tax is a priority for a retiree, perhaps keeping withdrawals from pensions to below the £12,500 personal allowance is a consideration. Other income could come from sources such as ISAs which are free from taxation.

Cashflow software can be used to show the long-term taxation levels by withdrawing money from varying investment and pensions pots.

Certain benefits can be lost when you access your pension and this should be considered before making any withdrawals.

Some pots are not included in an assessment should you require residential care. This can influence some retirees when deciding from which pots they will draw benefits.

Taxation can be complicated and if you are not comfortable with this area it's best to seek the services of a professional financial planner.

Reviewing the plan

Anyone in retirement who does not solely rely on income from guaranteed sources such as defined benefit pensions, state pension or annuities will have made some long-term assumptions about their retirement pot.

As this chapter has covered, these assumptions can never be exact and will be subject to change. For this reason, you should review your plan at least annually. The main aspects of your retirement plan that need reviewing are as follows:

Expenditure

How your own predicted expenditure has played out over the previous 12 months. Spending more or less than you have predicted each month could require a change in your strategy.

Assumptions

Be careful with this one. You will have to make long-term assumptions around a lot of factors such as investment returns, taxation and inflation. During your review it's unlikely that your predicted assumptions will match reality. But, your long-term assumptions do need to be long term. Adjustments should only be made when you feel the long-term outlook has substantially changed.

As an example, you may predict long-term inflation of 2.5%. At the time of writing, due to the impact of Covid-19, inflation is predicted by the Bank of England to run higher at 4%, but then to drop to 2%. [46]

Ultimately, you need to take a long-term view whilst not being afraid to stress test the impact of your assumptions being considerably different. A well-prepared retirement plan may have predicted a long-term inflation rate of 2.5%, but also stress tested the impact of 4% inflation.

Your income

Your income could have changed for any number of reasons. Some of your guaranteed income such as defined benefit pensions may have increased with inflation. The state pension increases each year in line with the rising cost of living as seen in the Consumer Prices Index (CPI) – measure of inflation, increasing average wages, or 2.5%, whichever is highest. This is known as the triple lock.

If some of your income has come from investments, perhaps these have performed better or worse than you expected.

Capital needs

You may have decided to get some work done to your house that you hadn't planned for. It could be your children are struggling and you have decided to help them out. Whatever the event sometimes we need access to capital beyond what we originally had planned for. In these circumstances it is best to use a cash flow projection and work out the impact of extra spending before you do it!

For anyone who has not planned this out, a reassessment of the retirement plan needs to take place.

Legacy

Perhaps your view on how much capital you leave behind for the wider family has changed? If it has, this requires a rethink of your spending habits in retirement.

Your health

A significant change in your health can result in your plan being changed. Any bad news regarding your health can change how you feel about spending money. In the past we have seen many clients make a recovery from poor health which results in a fresh perspective on how they live. Often, we will see clients choosing to live more for the moment and perhaps caring less about the long term.

This spending pattern is something we encourage, given our ability to spend money as we age can naturally be impacted by reduced health and mobility. But, this needs to be balanced with ensuring the retiree does not run out of money!

For those whose health declines and results in a limited lifespan, this can require a rethink of the investment strategy. Anyone who is invested in the markets should hold a medium-term outlook of at least five years. This is to simply ensure the retiree has the timeframe to ride out the fluctuations in the market. Should your health result in a lifespan of less than five years, consideration would need to be given to holding all your investments in cash. This would be particularly important if the beneficiaries of your estate don't intend to remain invested and perhaps intend to spend the inheritance.

If the markets were to drop significantly you may not have the time horizon to remain invested and fully benefit from any recovery. Investing in cash would seriously reduce the potential growth of your portfolio; however, it would also ensure the value is protected for your beneficiaries if required.

Financial services compensation scheme

Many retirees want to ensure their investments are protected in the event of a financial institution becoming insolvent. For peace of mind the financial services compensation scheme offers protection to consumers should a company fail. In 2008, during the financial crisis known as the credit crunch, many UK banks were under pressure and faced possible liquidity problems.

The crisis saw five banks failing, leaving savers stranded. The biggest name to fail was Bradford & Bingley. This alone cost the financial services compensation scheme

£15.65 billion! [47]

We worked in a well-known UK bank during this time. We witnessed first-hand the mass amounts of panic this created with UK savers. Many savers who traditionally used one bank to hold large deposits, moved thousands of pounds to spread their savings amongst several banks – the driver being to ensure that for every bank they deposited money with, the amount held would be covered by the financial services compensation scheme should that bank fail.

The current financial services compensation limits can be found on the FSCS website –

https://www.fscs.org.uk/what-we-cover/

Whilst these limits don't change often, they have changed in the past. Therefore, any retiree who wants to ensure their savings are within these limits needs to be aware of any changes made to future FSCS limits.

New products/charges

Financial services products available to the retiree continue to change. Like any industry financial services companies want your business. They apply charges in exchange for managing your retirement funds. These charges help them to build a healthy profit for their shareholders.

These products change as companies compete for your business. Typical changes involve either driving down costs or offering innovative options with contracts.

In addition, the Financial Conduct Authority continues to act as a public body to serve public interest by improving the way markets work and how financial services firm conduct their business. Through their intervention many new products are brought to market.

Stakeholder pension schemes were introduced in the UK on 6 April 2001 as a consequence of the Welfare Reform and Pensions Act 1999. They were intended to encourage more long-term saving for retirement, particularly among those on low to moderate earnings. They are required to meet several conditions set out in legislation, including a cap on charges, low minimum contributions, and flexibility in relation to stopping and starting contributions.

Through the passage of time our needs change. As highlighted earlier in the chapter, the number of people who use the internet has exploded since the millennium. This has seen increased demand for online access to investment valuations. As a result, many pension and investment providers now offer products that allow this.

New legislation

From time to time seismic changes in legislation can have an impact on your retirement plan. Anyone retiring in 2015 may have mapped out their retirement plan. Then George Osborne suddenly announced a radical change to pension options at retirement.

Pensions themselves have had other rumoured legislation changes that never took effect. One of these was in fact part of the 2015 review. It was proposed that anyone who already had purchased an annuity could now sell it in exchange for a cash alternative. [48] This was to be known as the secondary annuity market. In 2016, after engagement with the financial services industry and various consumer groups this idea was cancelled and deemed unworkable by the government.

I also recollect, in 2005, pre-budget proposals to allow a residential property to be held in a pension. [49] Again, this did not happen.

The most recent legislation change is around defined benefit pensions. A suite of changes confirmed in 2021 rolled out new rules and expectations for anyone who wants advice on the suitability of these schemes. [50]

On 7 September 2021, government set out its <u>new plan for adult social care reform in England</u>. This included a lifetime cap on the amount anyone in England will need to spend on their personal care, alongside a more generous means-test for local authority financial support.

This document sets out further detail on the workings of the new charging reform framework and confirms key outstanding policy details, including the standard level at which 'daily living costs' will initially be set.

The publication of this document also marks the start of a period of co-production of the statutory guidance with the sector, building on <u>draft regulations and guidance published in 2015</u>, and followed by a public consultation in the new year. It is intended that the regulations and final guidance will be published in spring 2022.

For those in retirement it's important to be aware of legislation changes and to look closely at the impact these have on your retirement plan.

Your general circumstances

Perhaps stating the obvious – your own circumstances can change considerably. The biggest change we encounter is the death of a spouse or partner. As well as dealing with the grief this can lead to massive changes in financial circumstances.

Reviewing your investment funds

For anyone not using an annuity, their pension pots will continue to be invested. The fund or funds they are invested in should have been carefully chosen. This should have considered several factors at the outset which continually should be reviewed.

- How cautious or adventurous the retiree wants to be with their money

Ultimately any investment strategy selected for your pension pots needs to be one with which you're comfortable. The level of long-term return needs to match your expectations. You will likely be disappointed if you expect your funds to grow by 4% and they only make 1%.

This needs to be counterbalanced with the acceptance that all forms of investment will have a downturn in difficult market conditions. The volatility and drops in value of any invested funds during these difficult times should ideally not be more than a level that you're comfortable accepting. This is an age-old trade-off between risk and return.

Through time, particularly as we age, it's not uncommon for retirees to change their own views on how the money should be invested. In our experience investors do tend to become more cautious as they age.

- The capacity for the retiree to lose money

You have established the type of investment that's right for your pension pots, balancing growth expectations with the potential volatility. It's important then to consider the actual impact difficult market conditions can have on your retirement plans and whether losses can be afforded. If not, the suitability of the chosen investment funds needs to be reconsidered.

- **Strategy of the investment funds**

It's certainly our belief as advisors that the strategy of your investment funds needs to be matched to your individual circumstances. For example, fluctuations in the value of investments have a bigger impact on someone who is continually withdrawing money from said investments. This is known as 'pound cost ravaging'. [51]

If you hold a retirement pot that won't ever be used to support your retirement – perhaps it's earmarked as a legacy for family – these funds won't be impacted by fluctuations in market conditions. Therefore, the chosen investment funds don't need to take potential volatility too much into account.

An example of pound cost ravaging – when income is being taken, the order in which returns are delivered can significantly impact the future value of the fund, even if the returns are identical but delivered in a different order. This might happen where units are being encashed to provide an income, as is often the case for drawdown.

Let's look at an example. Here, £275,000 is invested over six years and the returns from portfolios A, B and C are as follows. What you'll note from this table is that the percentage returns of the three portfolios are the same numbers, albeit arranged differently.

	Year 1	Year 2	Year 3	Year 4	Year 5	Year 6
A	25%	5%	20%	-15%	-20%	-5%
B	-5%	-20%	-15%	20%	5%	25%
C	25%	-5%	5%	-20%	20%	-15%

Below is the result if no income is taken – the colours of red, amber and green represent the worst, medium and best result over a given period. As no income is being taken after six years, the values are the same, despite fluctuations over the six-year period.

	Year 1	Year 2	Year 3	Year 4	Year 5	Year 6
A	£343,750	£360,937	£433,125	£368,156	£294,525	£279,978
B	£261,250	£209,000	£177,650	£213,180	£223,839	£279,978
C	£343,750	£326,562	£342,890	£274,312	£329,175	£279,978

When we introduce income, it is a different story altogether. The values continue to fluctuate but the end result is vastly different. Below is based on an income of £1,500 per month.

	Year 1	Year 2	Year 3	Year 4	Year 5	Year 6
A	£323,395	£321,081	£365,402	£294,090	£219,288	£190,815
B	£243,741	£179,009	£135,656	£142,892	£131,553	£144,087
C	£323,395	£289,717	£285,719	£212,591	£235,214	£183,430

So, why is this? Let's look at portfolio B as an example. This highlights the risk that with poor performance in the first three years, losses via income being taken are effectively being crystallised, and are thus never recovered over the time period.

By contrast, portfolio A has the best start and therefore gains rather than losses are being crystallised, so the end number is much better. Portfolio C sits in the middle.

This may have all sounded quite theoretical, until the Covid-related stock market falls took place last year, and then it became a reality. Fortunately, through stress-testing cashflow modelling many advisors had 'emergency' plans in place to cope with what turned out to be a relatively short-term depression in asset values.

Such emergency plans included:

- Running a cashflow model based on current circumstances

- Reducing the level of income being drawn

- Taking income from funds that may not have suffered the same falls, if available

- Considering taking income from outside the pension arrangement if available, even if only on a temporary basis

But what can be done to manage this risk within retirement plans from the outset? Well, there are several strategies. Here are some of the most popular:

1. Holding cash

It might be that an advisor uses a cash fund to pay income in the short term. Typically, these funds don't fall in value, so there are no fluctuations. However, an obvious problem here is that deposit rates are very low at the moment and in some cases almost non-existent. This means that although there is no fall in value for money earmarked for withdrawals sitting in cash, there is no growth either.

2. The bucket approach

The premise of this is that the fund is divided into a series of 'buckets' invested according to when the client may need the income. Used in conjunction with the first method, you may have cash in the short-term bucket and then perhaps two or three more buckets intended to provide income at points in the future. The general principle is that the longer it is until income needs to be drawn from the individual bucket, the more potential for growth there is.

This can work well but still has the problem of low returns on the cash element, and of course there is no guarantee of the other buckets providing the right performance for the earmarked timeframe. That said, a variation on this theme could be that a longer-term bucket is promoted to pay income earlier than expected, if it has performed well.

3. Natural income

This involves bond, dividend or rental income generated by a portfolio becoming the client's income. This enables an investor to avoid drawing on their capital or selling fund units, thus avoiding fluctuations.

However, this approach is not without drawbacks. Even if the yield (measure of the return on an investment over a period) is stable in percentage terms, when applied to the capital value it is likely to fluctuate. This means the investor's income will fluctuate from year to year.

This may not work if, for example, it is a retiree needing to budget around a particular income requirement. An example of how this could especially cause issues is the situation that happened last year when many companies reduced or stopped paying dividends (share of a company's profits). Of course, the investor could top up their income by cashing in units, but then you are back to the main problem of encashing units at the wrong time.

4. Smoothed funds

One final method is the use of a multi-asset smoothed fund. The fund can be invested in a wide range of different assets, providing an element of consistency of return. A 'smoothing' mechanism is also applied to the fund, meaning the unit price is only adjusted if the underlying value goes outside of set parameters. Otherwise, the fund will grow by an 'expected growth rate', which can also help give investors an idea of their expected outcome.

Typically, these funds remove some of the day-to-day volatility an investor in real assets would normally expect to see. However, they also have drawbacks. For example, the fund may not perform as well as expected over time or it may be that there is an adjustment to the value relatively soon after the investment because of a market correction.

5. A mix and match approach

Finally, one important point to mention is that none of these strategies are mutually exclusive. It might be that two or more are used for the same retiree to give them the level of certainty they need and ensure their capacity for loss is not breached.

Considering the range of options above at the outset of a client taking income, while also having an 'emergency' plan in place can help ensure this very real risk is managed effectively.

Whatever strategy is selected, it needs to be reviewed, and any investment funds will need to be changed should the overall strategy change.

- Performance of the investment funds

Any investment funds chosen to coincide with your investment strategy need to perform in line with your expectations. Clearly any investment not growing in line with your expectation or perhaps suffering heavier losses would need to be reviewed. Performance of your investments can also be considered against a benchmark.

Another aspect to performance is understanding how your chosen investment funds are performing against the wider market. In simple terms – how are your investments with provider A performing against similar investments offered by providers B, C and D?

The continued theme of long-term views again becomes important. Any investment funds you have selected should have gone through a robust selection process. This process normally takes account of several factors assessed over a timescale. As advisors we normally consider data of 5 years or more in terms of investment performance and selection.

Assessing performance of your investment funds differs depending on your choice of using active or passive investments. Passive funds reflect the underlying market they are invested in and your fortunes or losses as an investor are driven mainly by the markets themselves (see chapter 2). However, even with passive investment the choice is vast. Charges also do vary from one fund house to another. Obviously the lower the charges the better the return for the retiree.

Performance of investment funds with any element of active fund management will be more heavily influenced by decisions taken by the fund managers (see chapter 2).

When choosing an investment fund that's actively managed, we consider how the fund has normally performed over a 5-year term. Within this timeframe it could be that fund A has a year when is performs worse than B, C and D. If the fund has been selected based on long-term data, though, changing it due to lower investment performance over one year does not make any sense. There could be a reason for the returns being lower that particular year, which does not impact the performance when viewed over a 5 − 10-year term.

A five-year timeframe provides you with a much more rounded view and gives a better idea if the fund manager is adding value or not.

This can be measured by comparing the performance against a benchmark which is the industry average, i.e. how the fund is performing against the average fund taking a similar level of investment risk.

But, that's not to say you continually ignore poor performance. The key to reviewing investment funds is to ensure your decisions for selecting the fund at outset are also reconsidered as part of the reasons for removing it. If you selected a fund based on a long-term outlook and having reviewed that outlook now feel it's no longer suitable, then this warrants a constructive reason for change.

Buying an annuity in later life

Perhaps, like many retirees over recent years in the initial stage of retiring, you have chosen not to buy an annuity.

Generally, annuities have received unfavourable press in recent times due to the perceived lack of value. Given the lower annuity rates we face today, compared to the 80s when rates were so much higher, you can understand this view.

Annuities can be seen by some as a 'con'. This idea is fuelled by the risk of not living long enough to extract enough income during your lifetime relative to the amount of capital handed over to the insurer.

There are many other reasons why drawdown might be more attractive than an annuity:

- To take the tax-free cash and keep working. When you reach age 55 you might want to get your hands on the 25% tax-free lump sum. Any additional income you take from your pension pot while you're working could be taxed at 40% or more if you have income from a job or business. Because there is no requirement to draw money from a flexi-access drawdown pension, you can postpone drawdown until you actually retire and your income rate falls, and you'll have less income to tax.

- You keep your favourite investments. If you opt for an annuity, you generally have to sell your pension investments and hand them over to an insurance company. It's still attractive if you're confident that your own pension investments are actually going to perform well. But, your drawdown pension can enjoy the best of both worlds with an income and tax-free growth on the money left in the pension.

Annuity rates do increase with your age and may naturally increase in future years should interest rates rise. Perhaps in future years they may offer better value to the retiree.

Many pension experts argue that you should use your pension savings to buy an annuity because the income is more secure than drawdown. The problem is that annuity rates may be very low when you retire or if interest rates are very low as they are today.

One solution could be to start your retirement with a drawdown solution and make a phased exit by using part of your drawdown money to buy an annuity in regular intervals. If interest rates rise annuities start to become more attractive. There are no guarantees that annuity rates will increase in the foreseeable future though.

Annuities may appeal to older retirees who don't want the hassle of managing investments and desire what is close to a risk-free income for life.

They may also appear attractive to a retiree who is perhaps worried about how your spouse or partner might manage with finances after death. An annuity again provides a solution that needs no management.

For some retirees, as they take an income, the amount of capital left in their pension pot declines each year. This may be a pre-planned strategy that has been accurately worked out. However, this plan could fall off course if you erode capital, perhaps due to overspending or lower investment returns than you had accounted for. Revised projections could mean that you may run out of money earlier than planned.

For retirees who initially start with a drawdown and now find themselves in this situation, the solution could be to use remaining funds to secure an annuity.

With the introduction of new pension freedoms introduced in 2015, retirees may decide annuities are better purchased later rather than earlier in their retirement plan.

What happens if I can't afford to retire?

If, having reviewed your finances, it appears retirement may not be affordable, it's important to consider what sacrifices you could still make.

- Spend less income

- Spend less capital

- Leave less or no legacy payment

- Reduce your working hours rather than completely retire

- Release equity from your property, known as equity release – this requires a specialist advisor

- Delay retirement completely

Delaying retirement – how long to live to make it worthwhile?

We regularly see potential retirees delay retirement as their pension arrangements will pay more each month. Of course, at face value, having a higher income sounds great. However, what is regularly overlooked is the total amount you will get from the pension arrangement in your lifetime.

To illustrate, let's look at a pension that will pay £10,000 a year from age 65 or can be delayed and pay £10,500 from age 66. Although the £500 increase is helpful, by delaying 1 full year the retiree has missed £10,000 of income that would have been payable from age 65.

How long does the retiree need to live from age 66 with the additional £500 per year to make up the £10,000.

This can be a complicated calculation, but for simplicity £10,000 divided by £500 equals 20 years. It would take the retiree 20 years from age 66 to recoup the £10,000.

Deciding if it's financially worth delaying your income will be based on the extra amount you will receive by delay, and indeed how long you're likely to live.

Chapter 8

What Happens To Your Wealth When You Die?

"In this world, nothing is certain except death and taxes." Ben Franklin

How your assets are distributed following your death depend upon five main factors.

- You left a valid will
- You died without a will
- The asset was owned in joint names
- The asset was held in trust
- You owned a pension – these have their own rules

Death with a will

For most assets owned in your own name, who inherits these will depend on whether or not you made a will. If no valid will has been made, then who inherits these will be decided by the Laws of Intestacy (these will be explained shortly).

Making a will is something most of us are aware we should do. However, recent research by Canada Life suggested only 41% of UK adults have one. [52]

With retirement bringing about so many changes in circumstances, this is certainly an ideal time to make a will or indeed update your existing arrangements. Having a will can save a great deal of heartbreak and financial worry for your loved ones. Ensuring you have provided for them is important, but you need to create certainty that they inherit any provision you have made for them and a will is the one way to do this.

To make a valid will the following rules must be applied:

1. The person must normally be over 18
2. The person making the will must be of sound mind
3. The will must be properly signed
4. The will signing must be witnessed and the witness can't be a beneficiary
5. The will needs to be clear about what and how much you want to leave and to whom

Making a will is extremely important, particularly for any couples living together who are unmarried. I have regularly heard couples over the years suggest they are a 'common law partnership' and assume that each other will automatically inherit their wealth. This is not the case and in this situation the partner would have no legal right to assets unless a will has been made by the deceased.

Another common issue I have seen is retirees holding properties abroad. To ensure a controlled distribution of these properties, a will should be made in the country where the property is based. If you own a holiday home in Spain, you need a UK will to administer your UK assets and a Spanish will to deal with your holiday home.

Anyone can make a will. You can even draft it yourself. However, this is far from ideal particularly for someone with larger estates which could be subject to inheritance tax on death. A will not only offers the chance to plan for inheritance tax but also offers the opportunity to control who inherits your assets in future years. This is known as estate planning. 'Estate' refers to your property, personal belongings and money.

The most common example in this area would be a retiree who wants to ensure their assets pass to their children on their death. However, they worry about their child divorcing and the inheritance being lost in part due to this divorce. The implications in this scenario could mean their grandchildren ultimately inheriting less. A carefully drafted will can begin to address this issue.

I have met the occasional client who holds power of attorney for a loved one and presumes that will give them the right to handle the finances upon death. This is a common misconception, as power of attorney ends on death. It is a legal document that allows someone to make decisions for you, or act on your behalf, if you're no longer able to or if you no longer want to make your own decisions.

There are different types of power of attorney and you can set up more than one.

Ordinary power of attorney (OPA)

This covers decisions about your financial affairs and is valid while you have mental capacity. It is suitable if you need cover for a temporary period (hospital stay or holiday), if you find it hard to get out, or you want someone to act for you.

Lasting power of attorney (LPA)

An LPA covers decisions about your financial affairs, or your health and care. It comes into effect if you lose mental capacity, or if you no longer want to make decisions for yourself.

Enduring power of attorney (EPA)

EPAs were replaced by LPAs in October 2007. However, if you made and signed an EPA before 1 October 2007, it should still be valid. An EPA covers decisions about your property and financial affairs, and it comes into effect if you lose mental capacity, or if you want someone to act on your behalf. Although your existing enduring power of attorney still stands, with the introduction of lasting power of attorney you should consider reviewing these arrangements.

The person who will handle your financial affairs upon death if you have made a will is known as the executor. If you die without making a will, normally your next of kin will be responsible for sorting out your affairs.

Appointing an executor is not a decision that should be taken lightly. The duties of the executor can include the following and more:

- Dealing with the financial wishes of the deceased
- Settling any outstanding debts

- Registering the death
- Selling assets such as the family home
- Continuing the upkeep of the house whilst it waits to be sold
- Paying any inheritance tax that may be due on your estate

An executor can seek the support of a professional solicitor to handle these matters. Sometimes a retiree will appoint their solicitor as executor to remove the burden from their family at the time of death.

The following points are worth noting when choosing an executor:

- A spouse as sole executor is not a good choice, especially if they are elderly. Whilst some people like to keep busy when coping with the death of a loved one, others are in no state to take on these responsibilities.

- It's best to speak to any individual or company you have in mind before appointing them.

- Legally the executor must be over 18 and of sound mind.

- If conflicts within the family may occur due to personal issues or disagreement on how you have decided to distribute the assets, a solicitor would be a much better choice in these circumstances.

- If a family member is chosen, they need to have the time and ability to carry out the duties. This is particularly difficult if they live in another country.

Wills should be kept in a safe place and their whereabouts known. If your solicitor has made the will, normally they will store this for you.

Wills do need to be updated regularly. An area often overlooked is that after getting married your existing will becomes invalid unless the will stated it was made in anticipation of the marriage. Interestingly, divorce does not invalidate the will, only bequests to your ex-partner.

If you are excluding someone from your will who may reasonably be expecting to inherit assets from your estate, a note with the will explaining your reasons should be left. In situations such as this the individual who feels wrongly excluded can make a 'family provision claim' against the estate and dispute the will. A note explaining your reasons can help the court in such a scenario.

Wills are also vital for those with young children. The will can set out who should act as guardians for young children if such tragic circumstances should unfold. Children under 18 are legally not allowed to inherit assets. In such circumstances a Statutory Trust will be formed to ensure these assets are looked after by someone else until they reach 18.

So how does the situation change if no will has been made?

The Laws of Intestacy will apply

If someone dies without making a will, they are said to have died intestate. If this happens the law sets out who should deal with the deceased's affairs and who should inherit their estate. This person responsible for dealing with the estate is known as the administrator. This flow chart shows who your assets are distributed to should you die with no will in Northern Ireland. These rules change slightly for those in England.

These rules can also apply when someone has a partially intestate estate. This can happen for example if they leave a will specifically leaving their house to a named beneficiary but do not mention who is to inherit other assets. The assets not covered by the will fall under the laws of intestacy.

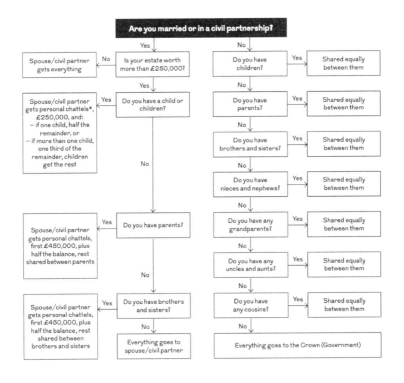

One area I find fascinating with this law is when a husband or wife dies leaving no will and the assets are above £250,000, so many people will presume that your spouse will automatically inherit all your assets. As this flow chart demonstrates, if you have children, they will share any portion of the estate above £250,000.

It's also interesting to point out that the Crown will receive the estate if no beneficiary can be found. The average estate unclaimed in 2018 was £150,000! [53]

A list of unclaimed estates can be found here:

https://www.gov.uk/government/statistical-data-sets/unclaimed-estates-list

How do you make a claim for an unclaimed estate?

If you believe you are entitled to an unclaimed estate, generally there are two ways of claiming for it:

1. Applying directly to the Bona Vacantia Division – members of the public who believe they are a potential beneficiary can review the list and produce evidence to support their own claim.

2. Using a specialist genealogist – genealogists are private companies who are experts in tracing people and persons entitled to inherit. They review the unclaimed estates lists and try to locate beneficiaries, usually taking a percentage of the deceased's estate as a 'finder's fee' when successful.

There are time limits for applying to the Bona Vacantia Division and no claims will be considered 30 years after the deceased's death. Claims will be accepted if they're made within 12 years from when the estate administration was completed and interest will be paid on money held. If the claim is made after that time, money can be paid out on claims up to 30 years after death, but no interest is paid.

What documents and evidence do you need to claim an unclaimed estate?

In any claim, you'll need to provide evidence, including:

- Your family tree
- Two documents of ID
- Any marriage, birth and death certificates
- Any other relevant evidence

If other relatives are also entitled to the unclaimed estate, they should be included in the one claim. The claimant has the responsibility to deal with the estate and make sure the other relatives receive what they are due.

Assets owned jointly

Bank or savings accounts

Where accounts are held in joint names the interest and ownership of the capital is split equally unless the taxpayers tell HMRC that it should be split in a different proportion. This would be done by completing a form 17.

(https://www.gov.uk/government/publications/income-tax-declaration-of-beneficial-interests-in-joint-property-and-income-17

By completing this form, the joint account holders are declaring that the underlying capital (which basically means the balance in the accounts) is held in that proportion.

For example, if I put £20,000 into an account with my wife, in the absence of any other information HMRC will assume that we each 'own' £10,000 of the capital and that any interest paid on the account will be split equally between us.

Should my wife and I complete a <u>form 17</u> and file it with HMRC, declaring that my wife owns 75% of the capital while I own just 25%, the interest would be allocated 75% to my wife and 25% to me. This would also mean that my wife was entitled to 75% of the balance of funds in the account.

Normally the balance in the account automatically transfers to the surviving joint account holder(s) on the death of one of the account holders. It is important to note that this happens regardless of what the will says. Should there be no will the laws on intestacy won't apply to jointly owned assets.

It is worth mentioning that ISAs (Individual Savings Accounts) are always held in single names. However, on the death of your spouse these can now be transferred to the surviving spouse rather than be cashed in, resulting in loss of the tax benefits.

What about other investments owned jointly?

Investment such as shares in companies normally follow the same principles as for bank accounts.

For investment bonds and other types of insurance policy, you will need to contact the relevant financial institution to establish its status. Although these may be owned jointly, they can be arranged on a 'second death basis'. This means that the contract continues when one owner dies and does not cease until the death of the second owner.

If we own our home jointly, what happens to it on death?

This depends on how the title deeds of the property show ownership. This is something that is normally set out when a property is purchased but can be changed later. The principles below can apply to other properties owned by the deceased, for example holiday homes and let properties.

In England, Wales and Northern Ireland, property may be owned as 'joint tenants' or 'tenants in common'.

Where it is held as joint tenants, on the death of one of the owners, the property becomes owned by the other joint owner. For example, Frank owns a property as a joint tenant with his mum, Sue. When Frank dies the property automatically passes to Sue as sole owner.

Where property is owned as 'tenants in common', each person owns their separate share of the property and on the death of one of the owners it does not pass automatically to the other owner(s), but instead it will pass through the deceased's will, or according to the laws of intestacy if there is no will.

For example, Christine and her husband, Ciaran, own their family home as tenants in common. When Christine dies, her will passes her share in the house to their daughter, who then owns the house jointly with Ciaran as tenants in common.

Assets held in trust

Writing life insurance or investments in trust is one of the best ways to protect your family's future in the event of your death. Your life insurance policy is a significant asset, and by putting life insurance in trust you can manage the way your beneficiaries receive their inheritance. In certain situations, investments are also put into trust, usually when trying to reduce an inheritance tax liability on death.

What is a trust?

Trusts are legal arrangements that let you leave assets to friends, relatives or whoever you pick to be your beneficiaries. A trust is managed by one or more trustees – family members, friends, or a legal professional – until the trust pays out to your beneficiaries, which can either happen upon your death, or on a specified date such as when a child turns 18.

Your life insurance policy or investments can be put into a trust, which is often referred to as 'writing in trust'. One of the main benefits of this approach is that the value of your policy or investment is generally not considered part of your estate.

How does putting life insurance or investments in trust work?

You will need to decide which type of trust is right for you. Your main options are:

- **Discretionary trusts** – your trustees have a level of discretion about which beneficiaries to pay when you're no longer around, using your letter of wishes as a guide. Your letter of wishes outlines your intentions as to how trustees should administer the trust.

- **A Flexible Life Interest trust** – is a trust where there are two types of beneficiaries. The first type of beneficiary is the default beneficiary. These beneficiaries are entitled to any income from the trust as it arises. In practice, if the life policy is the only asset in the trust there will not be any income. The second type of beneficiary is the discretionary beneficiary. These discretionary beneficiaries only receive capital or income from the trust if the trustees make appointments to them during the trust period. If no appointments are made by the end of the trust period, the default beneficiaries will receive all the benefits.

- **Absolute trust** – in this scenario, the beneficiaries are named individuals who cannot be changed in the future. This includes any children born later and a spouse following a divorce. The advantage of an Absolute trust is that the pay-outs can be made quickly without long legal delays, and as with other trusts, the inheritance Tax is likely to be nil or negligible.

Once your trust is set up, your trustees legally own the investment or life insurance policy and must keep the trust deed safe – they can ask a solicitor to store the documents or find a safe place in their home. Your trustees will ultimately make a claim to any insurer when you pass away, so they will need the trust deed close to hand.

It's worth remembering that on insurance policies, as the settlor (person setting up the trust), you maintain responsibility for making sure your life insurance premiums are paid. It may be beneficial to hire a legal advisor to ensure the legal wording of your trust agreement is precise.

Who can be a beneficiary?

You can choose any person, or people, to be your beneficiaries – this will entitle them to receive a pay-out in the event a valid claim is made. Contrary to what some people may assume, there are no rules that restrict who your beneficiary can be. For example, you could choose the following:

- Spouse or civil partner
- Child
- Relative
- Friend
- Charity

While you won't be able to change your beneficiaries if you have an Absolute trust, if you take out a Discretionary trust, your trustees will have the freedom to decide who your beneficiaries are, and how much they're entitled to receive from a pay-out.

The benefits of writing life insurance or investments in trust

There are many reasons why putting life insurance or investments in trust is a popular option. Here are some of the ways you can benefit from a trust.

- Control over your assets – if you don't have a trust, your money might be used to pay off outstanding debts. A trust gives you greater discretion, as you can decide who to appoint as your beneficiaries and trustees. Setting up a trust is especially important if you're not married or in a civil partnership, as otherwise your assets may not transfer to the intended recipient.

- Faster access to your money – without a trust, when you die, your would-be beneficiaries would need to obtain probate, which can cause delays. With a trust in place, your loved ones could receive the inheritance within a couple of weeks of the death certificate being issued.

- Protect your beneficiaries from inheritance tax – writing life insurance or investments in trust means the money can be paid out on your death and should not be considered part of your estate.

Cohabiting couples

According to ONS data released in 2020, around 60% of the UK population were living as a couple, and while many of these in older age groups were married, 69.2% of those aged 16 to 29 years were living together without marriage or civil partnership. [54]

While there is no legal definition of a cohabiting couple, sometimes called common-law spouses, it generally means to live together as a couple without being married. However, it's a misconception that common-law spouses have the same legal rights as a married couple, or as couples in a civil partnership.

As mentioned earlier the truth is that there are no cohabiting rules in law, and a surviving co-habitee has no legal claim on their deceased partner's estate unless the deceased left a will that includes their partner.

If you are living together without marriage or civil partnership, it's even more crucial that you have clear legal and <u>financial protection in place</u> for your partner and children after you die. With assets or life insurance written in trust, the proceeds can be paid directly to your intended beneficiaries, rather than to your legal estate.

Why pensions are different!

What happens to your pension on death is dependent upon the type of scheme and if you have been drawing any benefits. If you hold a **defined benefit scheme,** how these are administered on death both before and after drawing benefits will be covered in that pension's own scheme booklet.

However, these rules apply regardless of leaving any will.

Your pension administrator might pay a dependant's pension to:

- your spouse or civil partner

- your child(ren), providing they are under the age of 23 and in full-time education

- your child(ren) if they're mentally or physically impaired

- anyone who was financially dependent on you (or where you both relied on each other financially) when you died, including a partner you weren't married to or in a civil partnership with.

The pension they will get will be a percentage of the pension you were getting (or would have got if you die before your pension started being paid).

Any income paid to a dependant will be taxed as earnings at their marginal rate. This means they pay tax on money withdrawn from the pension at whatever rate of tax they pay on their own income.

If the pension payable is small, it might be possible to take it as a lump sum instead.

It's important you keep your pension nominations up to date, particularly after significant life events such as marriage, divorce, loss of a partner or the birth of a child. This is so that the trustees of the scheme are aware of who you would like to receive any death benefits that are payable.

It's important to note that although the trustees will take your expression of wishes into account, they have the discretion on who to pay the benefits to.

As stated earlier, any pension death benefits paid under the trustees' discretionary powers won't normally be included in your estate and so shouldn't have any inheritance tax liability.

Any dependant's pensions that are due are usually paid to the member's legal spouse or registered civil partner.

Some, but not all, schemes might pay the pension to a partner, with whom the deceased member was living when they died and who was financially dependent on the member. It's important to check with your scheme what happens when you die.

The lump sums below might be paid to your beneficiaries when you die. Generally, most pensions are set up under a discretionary trust. Where this is the case, it means the trustees have the right to choose who ultimately receives anything that is payable from the pension on your death. Where this is the case, it usually means that the value won't be counted as part of your estate and so won't be subject to inheritance tax.

You can usually submit a nomination form, often referred to as an 'expression of wish form' which allows you to tell the scheme administrator who you would like them to pay death benefits to. The scheme administrator doesn't have to follow your wishes, though generally they will.

1. Death-in-service lump sum

If you die while an active member of your defined benefit pension scheme, your beneficiaries might get a lump sum. This is often a multiple of your salary.

This is paid tax-free if the member died before their 75th birthday.

2. Refund of member contributions

Defined benefit pension schemes might also pay a refund of the contributions paid by the member if the member dies before starting to draw their pension. This is subject to the scheme's rules.

Interest might also be added to the refund of contributions under some schemes' rules.

Annuities

If you're in receipt of an annuity purchased through a defined contribution pension, what happens on death will be dependent upon the type of annuity you have purchased. The annuity is only payable to the person you named when you set the annuity up.

This is because the annuity would have been calculated based on your circumstances, including who you've nominated to receive the annuity when you die.

If you set the annuity up on a joint life basis, your beneficiary will continue to receive a proportion of the income you were receiving.

Be aware that if you opted for a single life annuity, the payments would stop when you die.

There might be further payments if you had a guarantee period and died within the guarantee period. In this case income will continue to your beneficiary until the end of the guarantee period.

A lump sum could also be payable if value protection were included.

If your pension is being paid, there's often a guarantee period (usually 5–10 years).

If you die within the guarantee period, a lump sum might be paid to your beneficiaries.

This lump sum is usually the value of the pension payments which are due to be paid between your death and the end of the guarantee period.

This is paid tax-free if you die before the age of 75. Otherwise, it's taxed as earnings on the person(s) receiving it.

There might be inheritance tax too, as these payments form part of your estate.

Defined contribution pension pots

You can nominate whoever you want to receive your defined contribution pension fund when you die. However, it's generally up to the discretion of the provider or trustees who look after the pension as to who it's paid to.

If you've completed an Expression of Wish/Nomination form, they'll take this into account. So, it's important you keep these up to date.

Again, if the pension scheme administrators have discretion over who to pay death benefits to, the benefits are normally free from inheritance tax.

If there's no such discretion then the benefits will be paid out to the named individuals in the proportions set out by you, but they could be liable to inheritance tax as these will have to be paid to your estate.

If no money has been taken from the pension when you die:

Your beneficiaries can usually withdraw all the money as a lump sum, set up a guaranteed income (an annuity) with the proceeds, or, they may also be able to set up a flexible retirement income (pension drawdown).

It's not always possible for your beneficiaries to use flexible retirement income to draw down from the pension pot rather than taking a lump sum or annuity. However, they may be able to move the pension to another provider to do this. You should check what death benefits different pension schemes offer.

If you've chosen to take a flexible retirement income and are in pension drawdown when you die:

Your beneficiaries can take the remaining money left as a lump sum, set up a guaranteed income (an annuity) with the proceeds, or, they may also be able to continue with flexible retirement income (pension drawdown).

It's not always possible for your beneficiaries to use flexible retirement income to draw down from the pension pot rather than taking a lump sum or annuity. However, they may be able to move the pension to another provider to do this. You should check what death benefits different pension schemes offer.

What happens if I die before the age of 75?

If you die before you're 75, anyone who inherits your pension fund won't pay any tax.

This is subject to the money being paid (or moved into another arrangement for payment as income or lump sums in the future) within two years of the earlier of the following dates:

- The date the pension scheme administrator first knew of your death, or

- The date the pension scheme administrator could reasonably have been expected to know of your death.

If you die before the age of 75, any pension that has not been accessed already will be tested against your lifetime allowance. As explained earlier the lifetime allowance is a limit on the amount of money you can hold in your pensions. Should you exceed this amount then the amounts above the threshold will be subject to tax. Once tested at this point, no further tests against the lifetime allowance will take place.

If a pension has been accessed and a guaranteed income (an annuity) or flexible retirement income (pension drawdown) set up, these will have been tested when set up and no further tests would take place before 75.

The lifetime allowance is the limit you can build up in pensions over your lifetime while still enjoying the full tax benefits.

For the tax year 2021–22, the lifetime allowance is £1,073,100.

The lifetime allowance will remain at this level until 5 April 2026.

If this allowance is exceeded, a tax charge must be paid on the amount above the allowance.

However, any pension that a beneficiary inherits won't count towards their own lifetime allowance.

What happens if I die after the age of 75?

If you die after 75, anyone who inherits your pension will be taxed on any income received as earnings at their marginal rate of income tax.

If your beneficiaries select to take money out through flexible retirement income (pension drawdown), they will only be taxed on any income they take, in the tax year that they take it.

There are no lifetime allowance tests carried out if you die after age 75.

State pension

Generally, when you die, your state pension will stop being paid.

There are a few situations where your spouse or civil partner might inherit some of your state pension.

Be aware that it isn't possible for anyone other than a spouse or civil partner to inherit a state pension.

The rules on inheriting a state pension are complex. They depend on what each of you have built up and when each of you reached state pension age.

Inheritance tax

Inheritance tax (IHT) is a tax on the estate of someone who has died, including all property, possessions and money. Even if there is no inheritance tax to pay, you'll still need to report the death to HMRC.

There is normally no tax to be paid if:

- the value of your estate is below the £325,000 threshold, known as the nil rate band (NRB);

- you leave everything above the threshold to your spouse or civil partner; or,

- you leave everything above the threshold to an exempt beneficiary, such as a charity or a community amateur sports club.

If you give away your home to your children or grandchildren, your threshold can increase to £500,000.

If the value of your estate is above the £325,000 threshold, the part of your estate above it might be liable for tax at the rate of 40%.

So, if your estate is worth £525,000 and your IHT threshold is £325,000, the tax charged will be on £200,000 (£525,000 - £325,000). The tax would be £80,000 (40% of £200,000).

When valuing your estate for inheritance tax, any liabilities such as outstanding loans are deducted when calculating the value of your estate.

Passing on a home

You can pass a home to your spouse or civil partner when you die, and there's no inheritance tax to pay.

If you leave the home to another person in your will, it counts towards the value of the estate.

However, the residential nil rate band (RNRB) can increase your tax-free threshold if you leave your home to your children or grandchildren. This includes stepchildren, adopted children and foster children. Nieces, nephews or siblings are not included.

There is tapered withdrawal of the home allowance if the overall value of your estate exceeds £2 million.

This table shows the increases of the RNRB and the potential combined allowance:

Tax Year	Nil Rate Band	Residential Nil Rate Band	Total for individuals	Total for couples
2021/22	£325,000	£175,000	£500,000	£1,000,000

It was announced in the Finance Bill 2021 that inheritance tax nil rate bands will remain at existing levels until April 2026.

Married couples and civil partners can pass on unused threshold

The NRB is fixed at £325,000 until 2026, but your NRB might be increased if you are widowed or a surviving civil partner.

Married or civil partnership couples can transfer any unused NRB to the surviving spouse or partner.

This can double the amount of NRB to £650.000. This extra transferable element is known as transferable nil rate band (TNRB).

Example

Jim dies, having made no lifetime transfers and left his entire estate to his wife Sue. None of the nil rate band was used. Jim left his share of the home to Sue on his death.

If we assume the nil rate band when Sue dies is £325,000, she would be entitled to a personal nil rate band of £650,000. This is because Jim's nil rate band was unused and therefore transferred to Sue.

Their home is valued at £400,000 so the executors may also claim the residential nil rate band. This will only apply if Sue is leaving the family home to 'linear descendants' such as children or grandchildren. In this case the executors of Sue's estate can claim an additional £350,000 of the estate that is not subject to inheritance tax. This would represent £175,000 of Sue's residential nil rate band and claiming the same amount for her late husband Jim.

As the home is worth £400,000 and the maximum residential nil rate band is £350,000, this means £50,000 would still be potentially subject to inheritance tax.

Note the residential nil rate band is always equal to the value of the family home on death but capped at £175,000 per person. In this example, should the family home have been worth £200,000 on Sue's death, only £100,000 could be claimed for Sue and the same for Jim.

How to value an estate

To value an estate, you'll need to:

- list all the assets and work out their value at the date of death; and

- deduct any debts and liabilities.

Remember to keep records of how you worked it out, such as estate agent's valuation.

HMRC can ask to see records up to 20 years after inheritance tax is paid.

Assets include items such as money in a bank, property and land, jewellery, cars, shares, a pay-out from an insurance policy and jointly owned assets.

Gifts also need to be included, such as cash or other assets, if they were given away in the seven years before the person died.

You'll also need to include any gifts given before this period if the person who died continued to benefit from the gift. These are known as 'gifts with reservations of benefit'. For example, someone gave away their house but continued to live in it rent free.

Debts and liabilities reduce the value of the deceased's chargeable estate. Think about items such as household bills, mortgages, credit card debts, and, in general, funeral expenses.

But any costs incurred after death, such as solicitor's and probate fees, can't be deducted from the estate's value for IHT purposes.

It can be complicated, so it's worth getting advice to help you make the right decisions.

Who pays inheritance tax?

If there's a will, it's usually the executor of the will who arranges to pay the inheritance tax. If there isn't a will, it's the administrator of the estate who does this.

IHT can be paid from funds within the estate, or from money raised from the sale of the assets.

However, in practice, most IHT is paid through the Direct Payment Scheme (DPS). This means, if the person who died had money in a bank or building society account, the person dealing with the estate can ask for all or some of the IHT due to be paid directly from the account through the DPS.

Sometimes the person who died has left money to pay IHT. This is usually arranged through a whole-of-life insurance policy, which remains in force until the policyholder's death (as long as the premiums are paid).

Payments from a life insurance policy could be subject to IHT. But, by writing the policy in trust, the tax should be avoided. This way, you also avoid going through the often-lengthy probate process.

When the tax and debts are paid, the executor or administrator can distribute what remains of the estate.

When do you have to pay inheritance tax?

If you need to pay inheritance tax, you'll need to get a reference number at least three weeks before you make a payment. This can be done by post or online.

Inheritance tax must be paid by the end of the sixth month after the person's death. If it's not paid by then, HMRC will start charging interest.

The executors can choose to pay the tax on certain assets, such as property, by instalment over ten years. But the outstanding amount of tax will still get charged interest.

If the asset is sold before all the IHT is paid, the executors must ensure that all instalments (and interest) are paid at that point.

If your estate is likely to incur IHT, it's a good idea for your executor to pay some of the tax within the first six months of death, even if they haven't finished valuing the estate. This is called payment on account.

This will help the estate reduce the interest that it could be charged if it takes longer to sell the assets to pay off the debts and taxes.

If the executor or administrator is paying the tax from their own account, they can claim it back from the estate.

HMRC will refund the estate if it has overpaid IHT when probate has been given.

If you've been appointed executor or administrator of the estate, you'll need to complete and send in an account of the estate within a year of the death to avoid a penalty.

Inheritance tax gifts, reliefs and exemptions

Some gifts and property are exempt from inheritance tax, such as some wedding gifts and charitable donations. This can be an area that retirees often find confusing.

Firstly, let's clear up one simple misconception: you can give away as much of your money as you like! There are no rules preventing you from doing this. I regularly meet retirees who are genuinely afraid of giving away their money for fear of breaking some sort of rule they heard from a friend!

Another common mistake is that when you give money away to your family, they can't spend it for seven years! Again, this is simply not true.

The 7-year rule simply means that upon your death, when calculating your inheritance tax position HMRC will include most gifts you have made in the seven years prior to your death. Providing your estate has enough money any inheritance tax payable upon your death can be paid from the estate and not the gift.

The following list of gifts are not included in your estate at death even if they are within the 7-year period.

While you're alive, you have a £3,000 'gift allowance' a year. This is known as your annual exemption.

This means you can give away assets or cash up to a total of £3,000 in a tax year without it being added to the value of your estate for inheritance tax purposes.

Any part of the annual exemption which isn't used in the tax year can be carried forward to the following tax year. It can only be used in the following tax year and can't be carried over any further.

Certain other gifts don't count towards this annual exemption and again for these you also don't need to worry about living for seven years after they have been made.

- Gifts that are worth less than £250. You can give as many gifts of up to £250 to as many individuals as you want. Although not to anyone who has already received a gift of your whole £3,000 annual exemption. None of these gifts are subject to inheritance tax.

- Wedding gifts. In this case, if the gift is to be effective for inheritance tax purposes, it must be made before, not after the wedding, and the wedding must happen, and it must be:

  - given to a child and worth £5,000 or less;

  - given to a grandchild or great-grandchild and worth £2,500 or less, or

  - given to another relative or friend and worth £1,000 or less.

- Gifts to help pay the living costs of an ex-spouse, an elderly dependant or a child under 18 or in full-time education might be exempt.

- Gifts from your surplus income. If you have enough income to maintain your usual standard of living, you can make gifts from your surplus income. For example, regularly paying into your child's savings account, or paying a life insurance premium for your spouse or civil partner. To make use of this exemption, it's very important that you keep very good records of these gifts. Otherwise, inheritance tax might be due on these gifts when you die. The rules for this exemption are complex. For example, these gifts must be regular. Grandparents can use it to pay for things like their grandchildren's school fees.

- Charitable gifts: If you give a gift to a charity, museum, university, or community amateur sports club, this is exempt from tax.

- Political party gifts: you can give an inheritance tax-free gift to a political party under certain conditions.

Any other gifts worth more than the £3,000 allowance and not falling into those described above will normally be included in the value of your estate if you die within 7 years of making them.

How can I reduce the amount of tax paid?

Trying to reduce any potential inheritance tax due on an estate is complicated. But, in short, you can reduce how much tax is paid by considering the following.

1. Spend your money!

It's such an obvious statement but most retirees have saved hard to build up enough wealth to support a comfortable retirement. Why not make memories with your family whilst you have the health and capital to do so.

2. Gifts to charity, church or sports clubs

In your lifetime or upon your death the value of these gifts is not included in any inheritance tax calculations. As an additional incentive if you leave 10% of your net estate to charity any inheritance tax payable on your estate is reduced from 40% to 36%.

3. Consider gifting money to your family in your lifetime

If you feel your children, grandchildren or indeed someone in your family circle could benefit from the money then consider this option. Should you live longer than seven years the value of this gift will be removed from your own estate for inheritance tax purposes.

Be careful before gifting money to your family, as once it's done you legally have no right to have it back. It's important to be sure you really can afford to let go of the capital without impacting your standard of living. Always consider what capital you may require should you need long-term care due to illness.

Before making gifts consider how the individual is likely to spend the money. Will it be used as wisely as you hope? Consider their own personal circumstances. Should they divorce, a portion of this gift may be lost to their ex-spouse.

4. Gift capital to a trust fund

As with a gift directly to your family, should you survive seven years the capital will not be included in your estate.

A trust helps deal with many of the concerns raised when gifting directly to your family. An arrangement known as a Discounted Gift trust allows you to remove the capital from your estate but you can continue to receive an income from it which helps support your own retirement needs. In addition, a trust can help put controls around how the capital will be spent by your family.

A trust can also offer protection from circumstances such as your family member divorcing, and part of the gift being lost.

In short, trusts offer a mechanism to remove assets from your own estate without losing complete control of who benefits from the capital and when they should benefit.

Trusts do have their own taxation laws which can be complicated and it's best to seek financial advice before deciding if this is the right option for you.

5. Agricultural property relief

You can pass on some agricultural property free of inheritance tax, either during your lifetime or as part of your will.

This can be an extremely complicated area and it's worth seeking a specialist tax advisor to work out if your assets qualify for this type of relief.

6. Business property relief

If you own a business, or an interest in a business, your estate may be entitled to relief from inheritance tax.

Not every business or interest in a business qualifies for Business Property Relief. Again, this is a very specific area of taxation and should you wish to check if your assets avail of business property relief you need to speak to a specialist in this field.

7. Maximise the amount of assets in your pension.

Inheritance tax can apply to any property, money and belongings you pass on. It usually doesn't apply when you pass on your pension money. This is because, unlike other investments, your pension isn't part of your taxable estate. That's why it's tax-efficient to keep your savings in a pension fund and pass it down to future generations.

8. Use a life insurance policy

Taking out a life insurance policy to pay some or all of an inheritance tax bill can make things easier on your family when it comes to sorting out your estate after your death.

It can help protect your home and other assets from having to be sold to pay an IHT bill, which must usually be paid before probate is granted. This gives you the peace of mind that you're not leaving your family and friends with a hefty tax bill to pay when you die.

Normally, IHT needs to be paid before probate can be issued. But where property is concerned, HMRC might accept staged payments until the property is sold. Or a bank might release money if it's paid direct to HMRC to pay an IHT bill.

A delay in payment can result in HMRC charging penalties and interest on the amount of the inheritance tax which should have been paid.

Most life insurance policies will count as part of the estate unless your policy is written 'in trust', which can often be done at no extra cost when taking out your policy.

This means that any money is paid out to your beneficiaries and not to your legal estate. So any pay-out won't count towards your threshold and won't be subject to IHT. This would avoid a lengthy probate process, so your beneficiaries will get their money much more quickly.

A whole-of-life insurance policy is often used for this purpose, which remains in force until the policyholder's death, if you continue paying the premiums.

How it works

- You set up an insurance policy.

- You specify the policy is held in trust. If you don't, the money from the insurance pay-out is counted as part of your estate and subject to IHT.

- When you die, the policy pays out to the trust, which might be used to pay all or part of your IHT bill. You might need to set out your wishes in a side letter to guide your policy trust trustees to use the funds in this way.

Estate and tax planning can be complicated, so it's worth getting advice to help you make the right decisions for your situation.

When is the right time to introduce the family to your advisor and why?

The dynamic of every family is different and there is no set formula when it comes to discussing money with your family. Having advised clients for over 20 years I have seen so many different approaches in this area.

The ideal scenario for a retiree is that your beneficiaries (normally your children) are financially independent and not needing any of your wealth. They make sensible financial decisions and generally have a stable family life themselves.

With beneficiaries such as these, it's best to involve them or make them aware of some of the financial planning decisions you are making in later life. This is particularly relevant when some later-life planning decisions are made for their benefit, such as inheritance tax planning.

Later-life financial planning commonly revolves around how best to hand over wealth to the family. This can typically involve protecting assets from inheritance tax, care home fees or children divorcing. Even later-life investments tend to be chosen with half an eye on ensuring a seamless handover to the family.

When your beneficiaries are aware of some of your financial planning decisions it can help ensure these plans are understood – especially if capacity to manage financial matters is lost at any point down the line, and it's then our children who manage the finances.

Experience in this area has also taught me that not every family has the ideal dynamic. Sometimes our children are not so sensible or stable when it comes to money. In some cases, the relationship with your children can be volatile. Occasionally some retirees can feel as if their children constantly look for support from the bank of Mum and Dad rather than earning their own way in the world.

In these types of relationships, it's more difficult and we caution introducing the family to the discussion.

Either way, it's best to discuss the family dynamic with your advisor and weigh up the pros and cons of introducing the family into your financial matters.

What happens to my assets on death?

Even if there is a will, sorting out an estate can appear complicated, many people use solicitors to take care of it. If the estate is small, or instructions are simple you could sort out a simple estate yourself.

What does sorting out the estate involve when the deceased left a will?

Sorting out the estate when there's a will means getting probate and distributing the estate as instructed in the will.

What is probate?

Probate is a legal document that allows the executor of the will to sort out a person's estate as instructed in their will.

If there is a will, in England, Wales and Northern Ireland, you will apply for 'Grant of Probate'. This is also known as a 'Grant of Representation'. In Scotland, this is called 'confirmation'.

When you don't need probate

You might not need to get probate if:

- the estate was held jointly with the person's surviving spouse or civil partner, for example a joint bank account;

- the estate doesn't include land, property or shares;

- the money held in the account is within the bank's limits. What this limit is and the policy for accessing it varies depending on the provider;

- The asset or life insurance policy is held in trust.

- Normally for pension benefits on death

In the above situations, you just need to contact the financial institution to let them know that the person has died.

They might ask for a copy of the death certificate as proof.

The surviving spouse can normally continue to access any joint accounts or investments.

Who should sort the will out?

When a person leaves a will, they normally would have chosen at least one person to act as the executor of the will.

The executor is normally a relative or a friend, or sometimes a solicitor or a bank.

It's common for the executor to be an heir of the estate.

If you're the executor of the will, you're responsible for getting probate.

To get probate, you can either use a solicitor or do it yourself.

Use a solicitor

If you don't feel up to the task or if it's a complicated estate, it's a good idea to use a solicitor.

It's also sensible to use one if there are doubts over the validity of a will.

You might want to think about using a solicitor if:

- the value of the estate is over the inheritance tax threshold and the estate is still earning a regular income where there are complicated taxes due. The threshold for the 2021/22 tax year is £325,000;

- there are doubts about the validity of the will;

- the deceased had dependants who were deliberately left out of the will, but who might want to make a claim on the estate;

- the estate has complex arrangements, such as assets held in a trust;

- the estate is bankrupt (also known as insolvent);

- the estate includes foreign property or foreign assets;

- the deceased lived outside the UK for tax purposes.

How much do probate services cost?

Some solicitors charge an hourly rate, while others charge a fee that's a percentage of the value of the estate.

This fee is usually calculated as between 1% and 5% of the value of the estate, plus VAT.

The table below is an example of how much you could end up paying for their service. This total doesn't include court or application fees, so the final bill will probably be higher.

Value of estate	Fees	VAT	Total payable
£100,000	£1,000 (1% of estate value)	£200	£1,200
£100,000	£5,000 (5% of estate value)	£1,000	£6,000

AN EXPERT GUIDE TO RETIREMENT

Some solicitors charge both an hourly rate and a percentage fee. But this doesn't always mean they're more expensive.

Most banks also offer probate and estate administration services. However, these services are often more expensive than using a solicitor.

Getting probate yourself

If you're prepared to take on the task of getting probate, you can save quite a bit of money.

You could then pay a solicitor for smaller things, such as checking through the probate forms.

If you decide to do this, be aware you're legally responsible for making sure that any claims on the estate, such as debts and taxes, are paid before the estate is distributed to the heirs.

You can now access the Probate Service online, so there is no need to download the forms. You can use this service if you're the executor and you:

- have the original will;
- have the original or interim death certificate;
- have already reported the estate's value.

If you haven't reported the estate's value, you can do this at GOV.UK

https://www.gov.uk/valuing-estate-of-someone-who-died

When you've completed your online application, you'll be told what documents you need to send to the Probate Registry. Most of these can be sent by uploading a photograph of the document, but the original will must be sent in by post.

Preparing for probate

You need to find the will and make copies of certain documents.

The deceased should have told you, a relative or a friend where they've stored their will.

Also check for:

- Codicil: this is a legally binding document that the deceased might have written to make additions or changes to their original will.

- Letter of wishes: this is a document that the deceased might have written to explain certain things in their will or tell what kind of funeral they want. The letter of wishes isn't legally binding.

You might need more than one certified copy of the following documents:

- the will;
- birth certificate;
- death certificate;
- the codicil(s), if there are any;
- marriage or civil partnership certificate, if the person was married.

If you're not applying online, you'll need to attach copies of these various documents to probate forms, and to access the deceased's bank accounts, investments or life insurance.

How to find the value of a deceased person's estate

Before you can apply for probate (or confirmation if you live in Scotland), you'll need to value the estate.

When you fill in the probate forms, you need to put in how much the estate is worth.

To value the estate, you need to:

1. Find out the value of any assets, such as property, private pensions, savings, shares, jewellery, or valuable collectibles. If you think the item is worth more than £500, get it professionally valued.
2. Find out the value of any gifts that the person gave away in the seven years before they died. You'll need to include these in the value of the estate. Certain types of gifts that were given away before the person died might incur inheritance tax.
3. Find out how much debt they have, if any, such as a mortgage, credit cards or loans. Include funeral costs as part of the debt if the estate is paying for the funeral. If there's joint debt, you'll need to work out how much the deceased's share is of that debt.
4. Work out how much the estate is worth when the debts are paid.

You'll also need to work out if they had any jointly owned assets, such as a bank account or a property.

Depending on how it's owned, you might have to include it in the value of the estate.

Value jointly owned assets

Before you can work out the value of the deceased's share of an asset, you'll have to find out how it was owned.

Examples of this type of asset are a car, a house or a piece of land.

They might have owned this asset either as:

- a 'joint tenant', or
- a 'tenant in common'.

Asset owned as 'joint tenants'

- both owners have equal rights to the whole asset.

- the asset automatically goes to the other joint owner if one of them dies.

- the deceased can't pass on their ownership of the asset in their will.

- you have to value the asset and include it when working out the inheritance tax.

But there might not be inheritance tax to pay on this asset if the value falls within their tax-free allowance or if the joint owner is the deceased's husband, wife or civil partner.

Joint bank or savings accounts

Joint bank accounts are nearly always held as joint tenants.

So, while ownership of the account usually automatically passes onto to the joint account holder, you need to value it as part of the deceased's estate.

To value the deceased's share of a joint bank account, you need to find out the balance in the account and divide it by the number of account holders. However, this might not be the case if the account holders have agreed otherwise.

For example, they might have signed a declaration of trust stating that the account is held by them as tenants in common rather than joint tenants. So, on the death of one of the account holders, their share as defined in the declaration of trust passes under the terms of their will or intestacy, rather than to the other account holder.

Asset owned as 'tenants in common'

- each owner can own a different share of the asset.

- the asset doesn't automatically go to the other owner if one of them dies.

- the deceased can pass on their ownership of the asset in their will.

- you have to value the deceased's share of the asset and include it when working out the inheritance tax. But there might not be inheritance tax to pay on this asset if the value falls within their tax-free allowance.

Not sure if an asset is jointly owned?

If the deceased owned other assets, such as shares, you'll need to contact the company:

- to find out how it was owned;

- to work out how much the deceased's share of the asset was and include that as part of the estate.

For property or land, if you can't find this information in their papers and records, you can get it for a fee, from:

- Land Registry for properties in England and Wales.

- Department of Finance and Personnel for properties in Northern Ireland.

- Registers of Scotland for properties in Scotland.

How to collect the deceased's assets

You can get access to the deceased's financial assets (such as bank accounts) by asking banks and other institutions to release the assets to you.

You should open a separate bank account for the estate, to avoid getting it confused with your own personal bank accounts. Opening a separate bank account will also make it easier for you to see the value of the assets and might also help avoid any disagreements between beneficiaries of the deceased's will.

The banks might refer to this type of account as an 'executorship account' or client account if solicitors are acting for them.

Safety of money held in an executorship account

If you choose to open a separate bank account, you should also consider opening it with a different bank to your own.

This is so you can be sure that any money held in the bank account has the full Financial Services Compensation Scheme (FSCS) protection.

While the FSCS does allow a temporary £1million deposit protection for up to six months for 'proceeds of a deceased's estate held by their personal representative', they can't guarantee this protection if your bank or building society goes bust.

The standard amount of protection is £85,000 per financial institution (some banks share a licence, e.g., Halifax and the

Bank of Scotland), which might be lower than the value of the deceased's estate.

https://www.fscs.org.uk/making-a-claim/claims-process/temporary-high-balances/

Working out inheritance tax

When you've got the value of the estate and how much debt the deceased had, you need to work out the inheritance tax due.

This tax is due within six months from when the person died. Interest is charged if it's not paid within six months.

To help avoid paying this interest, consider paying some or all of the inheritance tax before you finish valuing the estate.

If you're paying this from your own account, you can claim it back from the estate.

Applying for probate or confirmation

When you've valued the estate, you'll need to fill in a few forms and send it to the nearest Probate Registry office. You'll also need to pay an application fee to HMRC.

Paying off debts, taxes and distributing the estate

When you have probate, you have the authority to contact the organisations that are holding the deceased's assets, such as the bank or private pension provider.

Interest and fees will often stop for debts that are solely in the name of the person who has died once you've notified the creditor.

They'll ask for a copy of the probate or confirmation letter before they'll release the assets.

You can then pay the various debts (if any) and the taxes due.

When someone dies, their debts become a liability on their estate. The executor of the estate, or the administrator if no will has been left, is responsible for paying any outstanding debts from the estate.

If there isn't enough in money or assets in the estate to pay off all the debts, the debts would be paid in priority order until the money or assets run out. Any remaining debts are likely to be written off.

If no estate is left, then there's no money to pay off the debts and the debts will usually die with them.

Surviving relatives won't usually be responsible for paying off any outstanding debts, unless they acted as a guarantor or are a co-signatory of the debt.

If two or more people have taken out a loan in all their names, in most situations the outstanding debt will pass in full to the surviving people who took out the loan.

Distribute the estate

After you've paid the debts and taxes, you can distribute the estate as the deceased wanted in their will.

Write a final estate document

You might find it useful to write a 'final estate document' to show all the money that has come into and gone out of the estate, as beneficiaries and people owed money are entitled to request accounts.

This document should include a list of all the assets, liabilities (money the deceased owed to people and companies) and administration expenses.

It should also show the final amount of money to be distributed to people named in the deceased's will.

This document must be approved and signed by the executor of the will (you), and the main beneficiaries of the will.

Main differences sorting out the estate with no will

A person who dies without a will is known as 'dying intestate'.

The law decides who inherits their estate according to certain criteria called 'intestacy rules'.

If there's a relative or friend who is willing and able to sort out the estate, they can apply for a 'grant of letters of administration'.

This grant makes them the administrator of the estate and allows them to value the estate, pay any debts and distribute the estate according to the intestacy rules.

Sorting out an estate without a will usually takes more time. The family can instruct a solicitor to handle the estate rather than try to administer it themselves.

After you've paid the debts and taxes, you must distribute the estate according to the intestacy rules.

A surviving husband, wife or civil partner who was still legally married to the deceased can inherit the estate.

The deceased's children might also inherit part of the estate if it's worth more than a certain amount.

Close relatives such as surviving parents or siblings of the deceased could also inherit the estate in certain situations.

The flow chart earlier shows how the estate would be distributed according to the laws in Northern Ireland.

Chapter 9

Do you need professional advice?

"Price is what you pay. Value is what you get."
Warren Buffet

Introduction

There can be no doubt that choosing the right retirement strategy can be a complicated area. The complexity increases when a retiree has more pension and investment pots or when the value of the overall pots increase. There are so many areas to consider, making the wrong decisions can prove to be expensive. Not everyone will feel the need to take advice. Some have the confidence, expertise and time to make their own decisions.

This chapter is designed to explain the options available to anyone seeking help before accessing their savings and investments at retirement.

When you decide to take benefits from your investments and pension pots there are three main approaches you can take:

DIY option

You could make all the decisions for yourself. In respect of your pension, both defined benefit and defined contribution, your pension provider will send you a pack which outlines your various options. You can then consider these options in conjunction with your own circumstances and decide which is best.

Should you be in a defined benefit scheme you would decide how much tax-free cash you want to draw in exchange for guaranteed income. Anyone in a defined contribution pension who selects to purchase an annuity would carefully compare all the types of annuity and rates available across multiple providers before selecting the annuity they feel is best for them.

These decisions are irrevocable, choose the wrong option and there is no going back!

Should your decision involve moving your pension you would research and choose your new pension provider. You would arrange for this new contract to be opened and ensure your pension is successfully transferred to the new scheme. When the pension funds reach the new scheme, you would liaise with the provider to ensure any income or lump sum payments are withdrawn in a tax efficient manner. This withdrawal strategy and how the remaining funds are invested will be your own responsibility.

According to Liverpool Victoria, seven common mistakes made by retirees are as follows: [55]

Not knowing how much your state pension will provide

If you qualify for the full state pension, you'll be entitled to £175.20 a week (in the 2020/21 tax year), but you'll need to have contributed 35 years' worth of National Insurance Contributions (NICs) to get this amount.

You must have made at least 10 years of contributions to get any state pension. To help you work out how much state pension you might get, **request a state pension forecast on the government's website**. https://www.gov.uk/check-state-pension

Outliving your savings

If you take too much out of your pension too early, you risk running out of savings too soon.

"It's important to make cautious assumptions about your life expectancy and set a realistic withdrawal rate from your pensions, which will minimise the risk of your income becoming unsustainable in the later stages of retirement," recommends Martin Bamford, chartered financial planner at independent financial advisors (IFAs) Informed Choice.

The government has a useful tool to help you work out how you'll need to portion out your pension. https://www.ons.gov.uk/peoplepopulationandcommunity/birthsdeathsandmarriages/lifeexpectancies/articles/howlongwillmypensionneedtolast/2015-03-27

Taking out lump sums from your pension without proper tax planning

There's no tax payable on the first 25% of each withdrawal you make from your pension, but the rest is taxed at your marginal rate of income tax. That means if you take out big lump sums, you risk being landed with a hefty tax bill if the withdrawal pushes you into a higher tax band.

"Consider spreading pension withdrawals across different tax years to take advantage of your personal allowance and try to keep any taxable withdrawals under the threshold where higher rate tax is paid." says Bamford.

Losing track of your pensions

If you've worked for several employers over the years and, in each case, joined the company pension scheme, it's not always easy to keep track of all the different pension paperwork.

For help with tracking down your lost pensions, check out LVs handy **lost pensions guide.** https://www.lv.com/pensions-retirement/guides/lost-pensions

Exceeding the Lifetime Allowance

The Lifetime Allowance is a limit on the amount of pension benefit that can be drawn without triggering an extra tax charge. The current Lifetime Allowance is £1,073,100 (2020/21 tax year) and any excess attracts a tax charge of 25% if it's withdrawn as an income, or 55% if you take it out as cash lump sum. Find out more about the Lifetime Allowance on the government's website.

"Breaching this limit isn't so unrealistic for those who start saving early and achieve good investment returns – especially if they also benefit from generous employer contributions," says Patrick Connolly, certified financial planner at IFAs Chase de Vere.

"To put the Lifetime Allowance limit into context, for somebody aged 65, a £1 million pension fund is likely to generate an index-linked income of less than £40,000 per annum – hardly enough to fund a lavish and extravagant lifestyle."

Missing out on a higher pension income if you have a medical condition

If you have any kind of medical condition, such as diabetes, high blood pressure, or heart issues, and you plan to use some, or all, of your pension to buy an annuity or income for life, you should be able to get a higher income than those in the peak of good health.

"Annuity income can be as much as 40% higher if you qualify for an enhanced annuity," says Martin Bamford. "With low annuity rates, it's so important to secure as high an annuity rate as possible, so disclosure of your medical condition is a must."

Not taking account of the new lower Money Purchase Annual Allowance (MPAA)

The MPAA is a limit on the amount that you can pay into pensions if you've already accessed your pension benefits beyond your tax-free lump sum. The aim of the allowance is to restrict people 'recycling' money back into their pensions to take advantage of tax relief. In 2020/21 the allowance is £4,000.

"It's important to understand that some ways of accessing your pension benefits, such as taking your tax-free cash allowance or buying a lifetime annuity, won't trigger the MPAA, whereas others, like taking income from drawdown, will," says Patrick Connolly. "It is therefore very important that people think long and hard before taking pension benefits and understand the full implications of doing so."

Pensions can be complicated, especially with the many rules and regulations to get your head around. Getting expert advice will help you make the most of your pension savings – and really enjoy your retirement.

This chapter also contains a checklist of the key areas that a financial planner will consider as part of holistic financial planning advice. It would be important that anyone who decided to follow the DIY route has checked that they have taken into account all of these factors before making any decisions.

Guidance

For some retirees they are unsure if they need advice but feel the need for further information. You might go for guidance services that have been made available through the government and paid for by levies on financial services companies. You can have a telephone meeting with Pension Wise, a service which can be found on the government website MoneyHelper – https://www.moneyhelper.org.uk/en

Pension Wise is a useful service set up by the government offering a free phone-based or web chat service. A pension specialist can outline in broad terms your pension choices. It is not tailored financial advice. To qualify you need to be over 50 and not have any final salary pension entitlements. You can book an appointment online or by telephone.

We can also get an enormous amount of information and guidance from the internet. But remember, the internet is both a brilliant source of information and dis-information so you should be careful how you use it.

For many there is the possibility that you will seek the free guidance service and then realise you need to pay for professional advice, but hopefully will still learn a lot about your choices and options along the way.

The main differences between guidance and advice:

- Guidance will not provide you with any reports or recommendations. It can help you to think about what you might need to do, but it cannot replace specific advice and recommendations as to what you should do. An advisor will tell you exactly what you need to do and implement those recommendations.

- Under a guidance service no specific information will be obtained about your pension arrangements. The guidance provider will ask you a lot of questions to help you think about your choices and options. If you get financial advice, your advisor will ask you to sign a letter of authority. They will use this authority to obtain detailed information about your existing retirement pots from all your pension and investment providers. This could be important especially if your pension plans have hidden benefits such as guaranteed annuity or growth rates.

- When you receive advice, you will be presented with a specific illustration covering costs and charges, and risks associated with these recommendations.

- If you receive advice, this will include research throughout the marketplace and ultimately a selection of the plans the advisor believes to be best for you based on your circumstances and their professional judgement. Bear in mind, some advisors are independent, researching the entire market, whilst some advisors will choose from a restrictive choice.

- Financial advice will normally include implementation of any recommendations. Your advisor will work with you to complete any application forms that are needed as well as transfer forms required by your current pension plan provider. They will submit these forms to the recommended provider and ensure that the benefits are paid in a timely fashion. Under a guidance service you will not get this support.

- Guidance does not have any costs as this service is funded by a levy on the financial services industry. If you're getting advice, your advisor will charge you for their professional services. Most financial advisors will offer a free consultation so you can get to know them. This is also an opportunity for the advisor to get to know you and start to understand your personal circumstances. Any advice charges should be disclosed to you well in advance of completing any work. Prior to 2013, it was common for advisors to be paid commission by product providers. This is no longer permitted – today we charge fees for advice, in the same way as solicitors and accountants. These changes were introduced to ensure the advice you get is impartial and not influenced by varying commission payments paid by pension and investment providers.

Advice

For many, the worry of making a mistake with a lifetime of savings and complexity of options will mean they want professional expertise.

You may be asking yourself, are the fees for getting advice worth it? If having professional advice means less stress and worry and the assurance your finances are taken care of, then yes. [56]

Royal London recently produced a report specifically on this area. Since the Covid-19 outbreak 25 million people in the UK have experienced high levels of anxiety. They then spoke with 4007 customers. Before we consider the financial benefit of getting advice this survey confirmed the emotional advantages of seeking advice. Here are some of the results:

BENEFITS OF ADVICE FOR EMOTIONAL WELLBEING

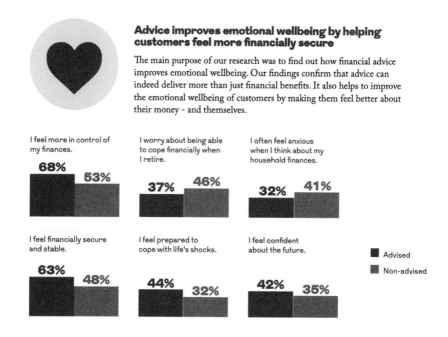

Advice improves emotional wellbeing by helping customers feel more financially secure

The main purpose of our research was to find out how financial advice improves emotional wellbeing. Our findings confirm that advice can indeed deliver more than just financial benefits. It also helps to improve the emotional wellbeing of customers by making them feel better about their money - and themselves.

I feel more in control of my finances.
68% **53%**

I worry about being able to cope financially when I retire.
37% **46%**

I often feel anxious when I think about my household finances.
32% **41%**

I feel financially secure and stable.
63% **48%**

I feel prepared to cope with life's shocks.
44% **32%**

I feel confident about the future.
42% **35%**

■ Advised
■ Non-advised

For anyone who decides to develop their own retirement strategy, it requires a considerable investment of time, and being sure the strategy will deliver what you want.

For those who are able and happy to invest this time, will it be done with the same knowledge and experience of a professional who has spent 20 – 30 years in the field?

Some of the tools we use within our practice carry considerable costs. For researching investment funds, we use specialist software to get data on investment funds performance. To produce cashflow forecasts over your retirement we use cashflow forecasting software. To consider the risk involved with any investment fund we use specialist risk analysis software. When giving advice we regularly use a compliance support provider to get a second opinion on what we do.

It is difficult to quantify the value of financial advice. Over the years, research has produced some interesting findings that highlight the benefit of taking advice when making financial decisions.

The Royal London study considers Office for National Statistics (ONS) research on personal and economic wellbeing in the UK. This study estimated that those who seek financial advice are £47,000 on average better off. [57]

When assessing financial value, one study found that individuals who receive financial advice were likely, on average, to receive 4.4% more per annum in net returns. This was through a combination of financial planning, preventing behavioural mistakes, rebalancing portfolios and tax advice. [58]

A good financial advisor protects you from making irrational decisions during difficult market conditions. I have lost count of the number of clients who panic in a market downturn and are seriously considering investments due to panic.

How much does financial advice cost?

Comparing advisor costs is important before selecting an advisor, but it's important to understand what each advisor does for the fee. Although financial advisor fees vary, the processes, knowledge, due diligence and value of what's included in the fee also vary significantly.

It's important to compare what and who you're dealing with, as well as how much it costs. Offering advice at a cheaper cost does not necessarily mean in the long term a better outcome for you as a client.

If you are interested in understanding the market cost of advice, the website vouchedfor regularly review the average costs across the industry. [59]

Vouchedfor is a company set up to support the public when trying to choose an independent financial planner. Not all financial planners are active or use vouchedfor, perhaps due to the demand for financial planners being high and a significant portion of the public using recommendations from friends and family when selecting a new financial planner.

Vouchedfor is a safe space where financial planners are vetted and monitored before being allowed to advertise their services. Once they are registered on the site they are rated by anyone who has used their services.

The cost of advice will differ between firms according to how they decide to price their services. Vouchedfor has searched its database to bring you the average costs of some of the most common financial requests. These should help gauge the kind of initial and ongoing costs involved.

Free initial consultation

Most financial advisors offer this to establish how they can help and must then make it clear what they can do for you and at what cost.

Taking out a £200,000 mortgage – £419

Among the advisors on vouchedfor who charge a fee for mortgages, the average cost is £425.

A £20,000 investment ISA – £1,359

£589 upfront, £770 ongoing management over five years.*

Investing £100,000 – £6,442

£2,577 upfront, £3,865 ongoing management over five years.*

Consolidating three pension pots totalling £250,000 – £14,265

£5,400 upfront, £8,865 ongoing charges over five years.*

AVERAGE HOURLY charge among financial advisors – £185

* Calculations assume average four per cent growth in the value of the investments each year. Numbers reflect average costs from more than 600 advisors.

Reasons why you may decide to get professional advice:

1. Understand your budget today and how this may change in retirement.
2. Keeping track of your budget, planned expenditure and assessing how changes to these can impact on wider financial plans.
3. Considering delaying retirement and want to know the advantages and disadvantages.
4. Worried you won't have enough capital and income to retire.
5. Understanding your pension projections such as your defined benefit statement.
6. Choosing the best combination of annuity, drawdown or UFPLS at retirement.
7. Improving your annuity rate and choosing the right type of annuity.
8. Selecting a pension provider for your drawdown or UFPLS.
9. Selecting the most suitable investment funds based on your individual attitude to risk and capacity for loss.
10. Help with minimising the taxation of your pensions and investments.
11. Understanding the features and benefits of your existing pensions and investments and whether they remain suitable.
12. Finding and understanding the value of any pension guarantees you may hold.
13. Choosing how much tax-free cash to commute.
14. Understanding how poor health changes the investment options and decisions you should take.
15. Worried about providing enough capital and income for your spouse upon death.

16. Worried about the impact long-term care may have on your plans.
17. Lifetime allowance issues.
18. Reviewing the assumptions within your long-term financial plan such as inflation, national average earnings, tax, interest rates, investment returns.
19. Deciding what order to withdraw from your pensions and investment, particularly considering taxation and any impact on state benefits.
20. Using cashflows to project forward the impact of your decisions on later retirement.
21. Ensuring your withdrawal rate remains sustainable if using a drawdown or UFPLS strategy, taking account of pound cost ravaging, sequencing risk and a future market crash.
22. Getting your money to work harder for you.
23. Protecting and maximising your legacy.

The benefits of an ongoing service

Once you have had your initial financial planning advice, you can continue with an ongoing advice service. This will entail a review at least annually and sometime more frequently. The average cost of these ongoing review services again is highlighted in the vouchedfor survey previously mentioned. The Royal London Report estimated that 61% of those taking ongoing financial advice services were financially better off.

As well as changes in your own circumstances, such as retiring, receiving an inheritance or an unexpected illness, external factors such as changes to taxation and legislation might mean that you need to adjust your financial plan.

Some investment portfolios will include changes to funds and be rebalanced on a six-monthly basis. A lack of rebalancing could result in both an underperformance of the portfolio over time and a change to the overall risk profile of the portfolio as asset allocations are not rebalanced.

Ongoing fees can be paid directly or by deduction from your investments. Ongoing services normally include the following, although this should be checked with your financial planner:

- Reviewing everything as detailed on the previous checklist;

- Valuations on your various investments;

- Taking account of taxation, ongoing due diligence of the products recommended and changes to your personal circumstances;

- Setting up or changing your income levels;

- Tax guidance when making withdrawals;

- Seminars on topics your advisor may feel are of interest;

- Regular newsletters;

- Support during difficult market conditions such as the COVID-19 pandemic;

- General enquiries regarding your financial affairs;

- Completing insurance claims.

Below is a checklist of the main factors that may change and drive a need to a change in your financial plan. These would all normally be covered under an ongoing review service with a financial planner.

- Changes to the assumptions you have used when calculating your retirement plan – e.g. inflation, national average earnings, interest rates, taxation rates, long term investment returns.

- Significant life events such as death, long-term care or declining health.

- Investment market crash such as the recent Covid Pandemic.

- Continued tax guidance when making withdrawals.

- Changes to your spending patterns.

- Changes to your views on how much of a legacy you wish to leave your family. Perhaps you want to gift money to your family now rather than on death.

- Changes to your need for capital, for example - extra spending on your home that you had not originally planned for.

- Change in your own income.

- The financial services compensation scheme may have changed and fewer of your investments are now protected.

- Potential underperformance of your pensions or investment funds which may warrant switching to better performing funds ultimately to improve your returns.

- Changes in legislation particularly within pensions and the impact this has on you.

- Performance of your fund needs reviewed.

- Charges on your investment or pensions have changed.

The following circumstances don't form a comprehensive list; however, they are common triggers requiring people to seek advice in later life.

1. One or multiple pensions assets and you're considering how best to access these benefits.

2. Total assets, including your property of more than £1,000,000 per married couple. If you are in this position inheritance tax is likely to be due on your estate following your death. There are some uncomplicated, wholly legitimate steps you can take to reduce this liability. Taking tax advice early on will give you opportunities to limit the bill.

3. Marriage, divorce, redundancy, death, retirement or inheritance. In all stages of life, these key events usually require a rearrangement of your financial affairs.

4. Drawing a large one-off lump sum from your pension. Remember that pension withdrawals are taxed as income. If you need to make significant withdrawals, for example to help a child buy a property, you may need to plan this to avoid paying higher rates of income tax. Depending on the size and complexity of your other income, you might benefit from professional help.

5. You have built up investments and pension pots and are unsure they are invested in a way that's maximising the return. It could be you're worried about the volatility of these

pots and have experienced significant drops in value. This is particularly topical at the time of writing given the market turmoil we have experienced with the Covid-19 pandemic.

6. You have worked hard during your lifetime to build up wealth. You're now becoming worried about how to pass some of these assets onto your family. You are concerned your wealth could be lost in care home fees or tax at the time of death. Maybe you're thinking of giving a gift of capital to your family now and are worried about how much you can give.

Where to find an advisor

If a friend or family member whose circumstances are similar to your own can recommend their financial advisor, start there. It's hard to beat a personal recommendation from someone you trust. If you're not in this position, there are several useful directories published by advisors, trade bodies or other organisations. These include:

- Unbiased.co.uk

An independent directory of professionals searchable by area and specialism.

- Vouchedfor.co.uk

An independent directory of advisors also searchable by area and specialism, but with the difference that advisors are reviewed by clients.

- Moneyadviceservice.org.uk

This is the government's general financial information service. It includes a directory of financial advisors.

Questions to ask when looking for a financial advisor

This checklist contains the main questions you should be asking when assessing whether an advisor is right for you.

1. Do you give independent or restricted financial advice?
2. What fees do I pay initially and how do I pay them?
3. What does your financial advice process look like and how long will it take?
4. How much do I pay on an ongoing basis if I want regular reviews?
5. What ongoing service do you provide for the fees paid?
6. How is your service delivered? Is it face-to-face or remotely by video or telephone call?
7. Do you have an office I can visit?
8. What level of professional qualifications do you have and are you qualified in any specific areas?
9. How long has your company been in business and how many staff do they have?
10. How long have you been working as a financial advisor?
11. Do you specialise in a particular area?
12. Will I always see you or can other people in your company look after me as well?
13. How often will you review my portfolio? Do you limit the number of contacts per year?
14. Do you charge if I need help making extra withdrawals from my investment?
15. Will you charge again if my investments change? E.g., if I crystallise my pension?

Important Information

The views and opinions expressed in this book are those of the authors and may not necessarily reflect the official policy or position of the firm that we work for. This book is for guidance only and the contents do not constitute personalised advice. Advice should be sought before taking any action.

Taking withdrawals may erode the capital value of the fund, especially if the investment returns are poor and a high level of income in being taken.

A pension is a long term investment. The fund value may fluctuate and can go down. Your eventual income may depend on the size of the fund at retirement, future interest rates and tax legislation. The value of investments can fall as well as rise. You may not get back what you invest.

Past performance is not a reliable indicator of future performance.

The information is based on our understanding of legislation, whether proposed or in force, and market practice at the time of writing. Levels, bases and reliefs from taxation may be subject to change.

The tax treatment is dependent on individual circumstances and may be subject to change in future.

The Financial Conduct Authority does not regulate Taxation Advice, Estate Planning, Inheritance Tax Planning, Cashflow Modelling, wills or trusts.

Any case studies in this book do not constitute personalised advice.

Appendices

1. https://ec.europa.eu/eurostat/statistics-explained/index.php/Duration_of_working_life_-_statistics
2. https://www.lloydsbankinggroup.com/globalassets/documents/media/press-releases/halifax/2020/halifax-first-time-buyer-0920.pdf
3. https://www.ons.gov.uk/peoplepopulationandcommunity/housing/datasets/ratioofhousepricetoresidencebasedearningslowerquartileandmedian
4. https://www.ons.gov.uk/peoplepopulationandcommunity/birthsdeathsandmarriages/livebirths/bulletins/birthcharacteristicsinenglandandwales/2018
5. https://www.ons.gov.uk/peoplepopulationandcommunity/birthsdeathsandmarriages/conceptionandfertilityrates/bulletins/childbearingforwomenbornindifferentyearsenglandandwales/2018
6. https://www.retirementlivingstandards.org.uk/
7. https://www.ons.gov.uk/employmentandlabourmarket/peopleinwork/earningsandworkinghours/bulletins/annualsurveyofhoursandearnings/2019
8. https://www.Aegon%20UK%20Readiness%20Report.pdf
9. https://www.hartfordfunds.com/insights/market-perspectives/equity/the-power-of-dividends.html
10. https://www.cib.barclays/news-and-events/2019-equity-gilt-study.html
11. Seigel, J. (2014). Stocks for the long run. McGraw Hill education. P5

12. https://www.morningstar.co.uk/uk/news/203214/do-sustainable-funds-beat-their-rivals.aspx

13. Hardin, A. M., & Looney, C. A. (2012). Myopic loss aversion: Demystifying the key factors influencing decision problem framing. Organizational Behaviour and Human Decision Processes, 117(2), 311–331.

14. https://www.investec.com/en_gb/focus/coronavirus/daniel-crosby-how-covid-19-will-change-the-way-we-invest.html

15. https://am.jpmorgan.com/us/en/asset-management/liq/insights/market-insights/portfolio-considerations-for-investors-concerned-about-a-downturn/

16. Source: Fidelity International Period: 31/12/04 - 31/12/19

17. Source: Lipper IM: 31/12/85 to 31/10/18

18. Miccolis, J.A. and D.R. Perrucci (2009). Asset allocation for dummies. John Wiley & Sons, Inc. P13.

19. https://www.hl.co.uk/news/articles/archive/my-house-is-my-pension.-the-pension-vs-property-debate

20. https://sevencapital.com/uk-property-investment/best-rental-yields-uk/

21. siblisresearch.com/data/ftse-all-total-return-dividend

22. https://www.ons.gov.uk/peoplepopulationandcommunity/birthsdeathsandmarriages/ageing/articles/howwouldyousupportourageingpopulation/2019-06-24

23. https://www.payingforcare.org/how-much-does-care-cost/

24. The LaingBuisson Care of Older People Report 2019

25. https://www.thisismoney.co.uk/money/guides/article-8262835/Best-money-management-apps-track-finances.html

26. https://bridebook.co.uk/article/bridebook-wedding-report-2020

27. https://www.legalandgeneralgroup.com/media/17339/bank-of-mum-and-dad-2019-a4-20pp.pdf

28. https://www.resolutionfoundation.org/app/uploads/2018/04/Home-improvements.pdf

29. https://www.parkdeanresorts.co.uk/holidays/top-bucket-list-ideas-2021/

30. https://ilcuk.org.uk/understanding-retirement-journeys-expectations-vs-reality/

31. https://www.resolutionfoundation.org/publications/the-million-dollar-be-question-inheritances-gifts-and-their-implications-for-generational-living-standards/

32. https://www.royallondon.com/media/policy-papers/

33. https://www.ons.gov.uk/peoplepopulationandcommunity/birthsdeathsandmarriages/lifeexpectancies/bulletins/pastandprojecteddatafromtheperiodandcohortlifetables/1981to2068

34. https://www.ftadviser.com/2014/03/19/pensions/personal-pensions/budget-no-one-will-have-to-buy-an-annuity-cRXtzQyqSVju3hk-Gy22aoM/article.html

35. https://www.bbc.co.uk/news/uk-politics-26649162

36. https://www.investorschronicle.co.uk/managing-your-money/2020/09/24/when-is-an-annuity-appropriate/

37. https://bandce.co.uk/wp-content/uploads/2016/03/ssga-tpp-report-new-choices-big-decisions.pdf & https://www.weforum.org/minding-the-400-trillion-pensions-gap

38. https://www.actionfraud.police.uk/news/pension-savers-claim-over-30-million-lost-to-scams-as-regulators-urge-footie-fans-to-show-scammers-the-red-card

39. https://www.nerdwallet.com/article/investing/inflation-calculator

40. http://www.candidmoney.com/calculators/historic-inflation-calculator

41. https://en.wikipedia.org/wiki/Open_Market_Option#:~:text=The%20Open%20Market%20Option%20(or,offered%20by%20their%20pension%20provider.

42. http://www.candidmoney.com/calculators/inflation-impact-calculator

43. https://www.gov.uk/government/news/new-pension-tracing-service-website-launched

44. https://www.candidmoney.com/calculators/historic-inflation-calculator

45. https://www.bankofengland.co.uk/boeapps/database/Bank-Rate.asp

46. https://en.wikipedia.org/wiki/History_of_taxation_in_the_United_ Kingdom#:~:text=In%20the%20first%20budget%20after,40%25%20 in%20the%201988%20budget.
47. https://www.brooksmacdonald.com/learning-zone/decumulation/ sequencing-risk
48. https://www.bbc.co.uk/news/business-58098118
49. https://www.fscs.org.uk/media/press/2018/sep/10-years-after-failures/
50. https://www.gov.uk/government/news/pension-freedoms-to-be-extended-to-people-with-annuities
51. https://www.theguardian.com/business/2005/dec/05/ prebudgetreport.politics
52. https://www.fca.org.uk/news/news-stories/fca-confirms-finalised-guidance-advising-defined-benefit-transfers
53. https://www.moneymarketing.co.uk/analysis/five-ways-to-manage-sequence-of-return-risk-in-drawdown/
54. https://www.wealthadviser.co/2020/09/28/290151/thirty-one-million-uk-adults-dont-have-will-place-says-new-research
55. https://www.co-oplegalservices.co.uk/media-centre/articles-may-aug-2018/over-9000-unclaimed-estates-in-the-uk/
56. https://www.ons.gov.uk/peoplepopulationandcommunity/populatio-nandmigration/populationestimates/bulletins/populationestimates-bymaritalstatusandlivingarrangements/2019
57. https://www.lv.com/pensions-retirement/common-pension-pitfalls
58. https://adviser.royallondon.com/globalassets/docs/adviser/ misc/brp8pd0009-feeling-the-benefit-of-financial-advice-customer-report.pdf
59. https://ilcuk.org.uk/financial-advice-provides-47k-wealth-uplift-in-decade/
60. https://russellinvestments.com/-/media/files/au/support/business-solutions/practice-management/value-of-adviser/2019-value-of-an-adviser_adviser-report.pdf
61. https://2021guide.vouchedfor.co.uk/cost-of-advice